How to Score
from First Base!
(In Sales)

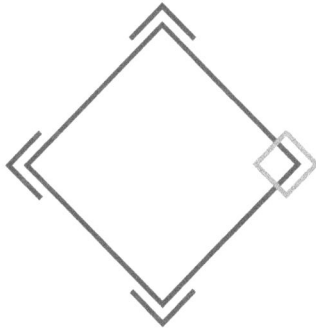

A Step-by-Step Guide to Shorten
Sales Cycles and Multiply Revenue

RAY RUECKER

To Kate, Olivia, and William,
whose endless love and support made this possible
(even in the middle of a pandemic.)

To my parents, Arnold and Fran Ruecker,
a million thank yous could never be enough.
I love you.

IN PRAISE...

"I worked with Ray Ruecker and his Connect 5000 team for nearly two years at Talari before the firm's Oracle acquisition. Connect 5000's sales development reps acted seamlessly as Talari's inside sales team in a highly-competitive multi-billion Software-Defined WAN market. Talari didn't staff this sales function internally and our team collaborated with Connect 5000 to drive a large percentage of sales meetings impacting the bottom line. Ray and the Connect 5000 team were consummate professionals in all facets and I thoroughly enjoyed working with them. His team consistently provided Talari with tangible results needed to fill the top of the funnel for our outside sales team and drive revenue. Ray is skilled at account-based and category-based lead generation, business development, and inside sales and I highly recommend the proactive inclusion of Ray's easy to follow sales development principles from his book." – **Adam Stein,** *Principal, APS Marketing*

"When I was the Chief Marketing Officer at Xangati, I used Connect 5000 and Ray Ruecker's team to do lead generation for several months and was pleased. After Virtual Instruments acquired us, I moved to two other firms in the same role. I reached out to Connect 5000 and have been partnering with his team again and again for business development and lead generation efforts and highly recommend his services."
– **Atchison Frazer,** *Worldwide Head of Marketing, 3X Client*

"Ray and his team at Connect 5000 uncovered great leads for us and were able to put my team in touch with some excellent opportunities. They did what they said they were going to do." – **Gary Greenberger,** *Vice President of Global Sales, 2X Client*

"Ray is a top-notch inside sales leader. He knows how to manage his team to work diligently towards results. He is very creative with his calling approach and works hard to define the best process to get the prospects to engage with him. His approach was how our firm found him and our busy SVP of Sales brought him in." – **Gretchen Hoffman,** *Senior Director, Global Marketing & Demand Generation*

"Ray is the only choice for me when it comes to developing effective outbound strategies. I don't make referrals lightly, but I can say with certainty I can recommend any of my clients to Ray and know they will be treated with integrity and Ray will get the job done." – **Lance Cleaver,** *Vice President*

"My company hired Ray Ruecker to help my sales team prospect and get into companies more quickly and efficiently. He spent almost a day with us conducting a hands-on workshop on how to be more effective in this sales process. I liked his fresh and creative approaches and I took a lot of ideas from him. I highly recommend attending his workshop. You won't be disappointed or bored." – **Ben Bianchino**

"I have had the pleasure to work with Ray at Connect 5000. My sales team and I attended a two-day workshop led by Ray that taught us how to better research and communicate with high-value potential clients. Ray is highly effective as a communicator and instructor, and will add value to anyone/team interested in learning how to use technology and proven communications tools and methods to reach new clients and increase sales." – **Charles A. Parsons II**

"Ray is an expert at connecting with key decision-makers and opening up constructive dialogues. I've seen it firsthand, and I've also interviewed his clients who enthusiastically recommend him and his work. Ray is generous with clients, colleagues, and fellow entrepreneurs and also happens to be one of the smartest and nicest people you will meet. Ray delivers new business development results and he does it efficiently and effectively." – **John Stevenson,** *Owner, Client Kudos*

"In today's highly competitive environment Ray Ruecker is an invaluable resource. Ray removes obstacles; he engages, connects, and communicates a value proposition with laser-like precision. His combination of charm and grit is expressed through his eloquence. Key decision-makers stand up and take notice when Ray calls, I would recommend Ray to any organization that is grappling with how to optimize their resources to break into key accounts. He not only opens the door...he gets you a place at the table." – **Keith Sciulli,** *Vice President*

TABLE *of* CONTENTS

PREFACE

"Connectors are people who link us up with the world.
People with a special gift for bringing the world together."
– Malcolm Gladwell, *The Tipping Point*

Connector.

If you could only use one word to describe me, this would be me in a nutshell. Nicknamed *"The Resource"* by countless family and friends, I've always had a passion for bringing people together. If I can't personally help you, then chances are I know someone who can. This knack for connecting extends not only into the business world but also into life and love as well. Of the five couples I've introduced, three ended up engaged and two are now married. It isn't always that our personal and professional calling align. But in my case, my natural ability for connecting people socially, personally, and even spiritually established the foundation for my career path and the creation of my company, Connect 5000.

In many ways, the genesis of Connect 5000 came about accidentally. As I became more and more adept at bringing others together, I realized I could earn a living connecting people. It was as though my passion, mission, and vocation came together all at once. It came about simply by identifying something I loved was something the world needed and in turn, could be monetized. Harvey Mackay once said, *"Find something you love to do and you'll never have to work a day in your life."* For me, the process of connecting people has rarely seemed like work. In that, I am extremely fortunate.

But how does my professional journey relate to this concept of scoring from first base? Once again, the answer is through connection. Sales have been and always will be about people connecting with other people and consists of two main parts: Getting in the door and closing the deal. You can't have one without the other, especially with high average sales and long sales cycles. While there is an abundance of sales experts who will tell you what you should do, there are very few who will tell you how to do it, step-by-step. Just as many will tell you what to do once you are already on a sales call, but then bypass how to effectively get in the door of targeted companies.

The same goes for constructive sales wisdom, strategy, and advice. There is a vast amount of authors who offer inspiration and encouragement for those who need focus and direction. Think along the lines of Jeb Blount, Mark Hunter, Anthony Iannarino, Jill Konrath, Andy Paul, Art Sobczak, Mike Weinberg, and Zig Ziglar. All produce critically important content in an oversaturated category, which is why this book isn't about inspiration, closing the sale, or getting the deal.

This book is intended for CEOs and Vice Presidents of software, technology, or consulting firms with high average sales who are in charge of marketing, lead generation, inside sales, or generating B2B sales revenue. If you're self-employed and/or work for a small professional services firm without a marketing department, this book is for you. While countless books will tell you how to effectively sell once you're already in the door, the real challenge is making that initial connection, getting the first meeting, and eventually scoring from first base.

Let's consider the game of baseball for a moment. While it has plenty of nuances and strategic moves within the contest, the rules of scoring are simple and straightforward. Whether you smack a double or drill a home run, you have to touch first base before you can make your way to home plate for the run to count on the scoreboard. It doesn't matter if you steal every base or if your teammates bring you safely home, you have to touch every base for the run to count. In sales, the same concept applies. For our purposes, each base represents a step needed to close the sale. Those steps correlate to bases in the following way:

1st base: Getting the first initial meeting with a prospect or referral.

2nd base: Having a quality discovery discussion to determine whether or not you are a good fit for one another.

3rd base: Preparing and sending a proposal to the prospect or referral.

Home Plate: Converting the prospect to a paying client when he/she signs on the dotted line.

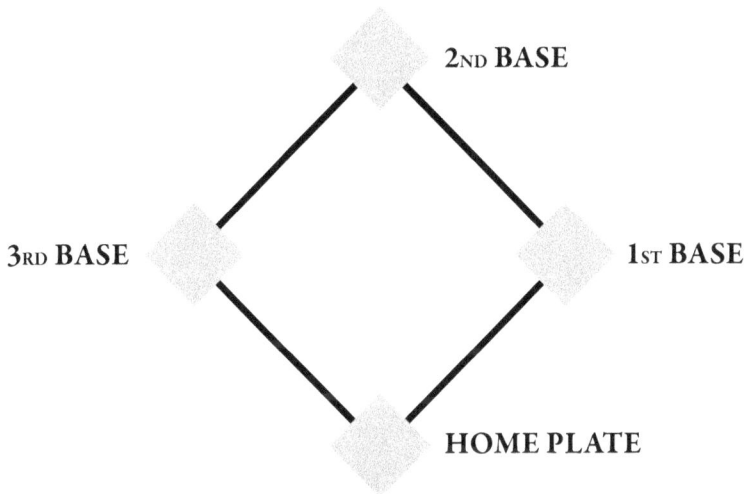

2ND **BASE**

3RD **BASE**   1ST **BASE**

HOME PLATE

Keep in mind that it is very rare for this to happen in one call. But it's also important to note that I said rarely, so be prepared for the exception. No matter how quickly you make it to home plate, the key to scoring begins with getting to first base.

Getting on first base is known by many other names, including business development, lead generation, and the most dreaded name of all, cold calling. No matter how it's labeled, prospecting and connecting must be part of your daily routine if you're responsible for getting in the door at targeted companies. For whatever reason, the term "calling" seems to have negative connotations, which is why I prefer using the word "connecting" because it fits the true spirit of the exercise. With such a vast array of terminology attached to this practice, you might ask, "Do we need another book on sales connecting?" The answer is a firm, "Yes."

But why should you take advice from me?

Since August 2006, I've been in the business of connecting people professionally as a self-employed entrepreneur. Over time, I have built a team of inside sales representatives on an outsourced basis for various software, technology, and consulting firms across the United States. I've never taken venture capital money and have always self-funded my company solely with my connecting efforts. My mantra is the more prospects I meet, the more opportunities I'll uncover. While I can't control the weather, economy, company decisions, timing, or luck, I can control my sales activity and work effort.

It is out of this experience and philosophy that this book was written. It was purposefully designed to provide you with a blueprint that shortens sales cycles and multiplies revenue. In every way, it's a sales playbook that creates a foundation on which to build upon and tweak for your organization. I won't just tell you what to do, I'll show you how to do it step-by-step.

If you are looking for a magic pill or Tony-Robbins-like motivation, this probably isn't for you. Because the truth is if you're in sales, you should already be self-motivated and understand that motivation from external sources will be short-lived. But if you're interested in practical and purposeful ways to connect with prospects that eventually turn into sales, this book *is* for you. And while it's true that sales connecting can initially be hard work, the more time that passes, the easier connecting becomes. Simply put, it's a journey that takes dedication, discipline, and long-term consistency. But it's one that ends with sustainable success.

INTRODUCTION

"Results are the harvest that comes from our past efforts." - Jim Rohn

Take a minute to visualize a three-legged wooden bar stool--the kind that greets you during happy hour at your favorite restaurant or bar. Now take that image and imagine that the three legs that support you are now the three legs that support successful lead generation. Each one represents the individual tasks guaranteeing success through cultivating inbound marketing leads, generating referrals/networking, and proactively outbound calling and connecting.

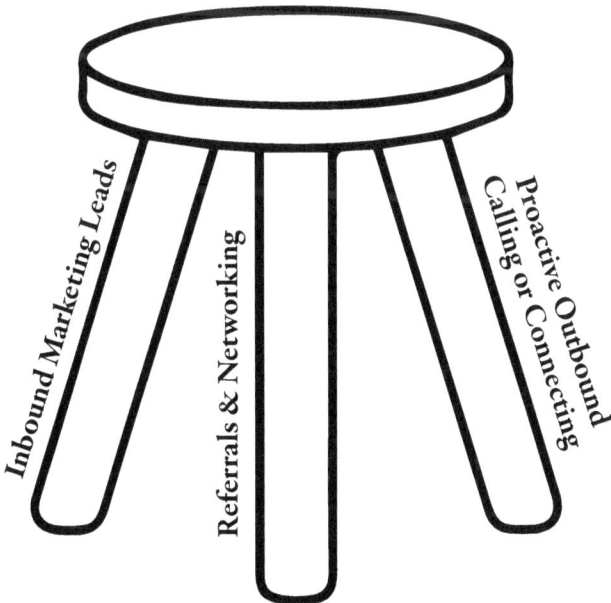

Each task includes any marketing activity motivating a prospect to raise his/her hand to say "I'm interested, tell me more." And while it may seem that I'm being overly broad in my description, stay engaged for a moment. Since lead generation can take many forms, including phone calls, email, direct mail, content marketing, etc., it can sometimes be difficult to simplify and categorize. But when you whittle it all down, each type fits neatly into one of these three "legs" or subcategories.

Leg #1: Inbound Marketing Leads

If you're fortunate enough to work for a company that has a marketing department that feeds you an abundance of inbound leads, congratulations. Trust me, I don't mean that sarcastically. All things being equal, I'd rather receive warm inbound leads where a prospect has reached out to me over trying to connect with a prospect who's never heard of me or my company. We should all gather as many qualified leads as possible.

But here's the problem with relying exclusively on inbound leads: You can't control the number of inbound leads that you or your sales team will receive. Marketing success goes up and down, often for no apparent rhyme or reason. Consider what might happen to your pipeline if your company eliminates its marketing department. (Something that occurs far more often than you might think.) This can come as a result of layoffs, corporate mergers, recession, COVID-19, etc. AdAge cites that the average tenure of a Chief Marketing Officer is 4 years--about the same length as a presidential term.[1] Of course, if you're receiving more leads than necessary to keep your pipeline full of quality opportunities, feel free to ignore me and put this book down. But know that while I've worked with a few clients who have built a robust lead generation machine, most companies have yet to achieve the same.

Leg #2: Referrals and Networking

If you have a golden Rolodex or unlimited LinkedIn connections that have been built and maintained over your career, well done. Again, I say this with all sincerity. Having those networks and connections are priceless and will always be the best method for generating new business. Because referrals are the ideal way to increase your credibility and get you in the door quickly to connect with prospective clients.

But here's the problem with exclusively relying on referrals and networking: Much like inbound leads, you can't control the number of introductions you'll receive from your past and present clients. You also can't control the number of connections your social network will make on your behalf, even if you're asking for them. People are busy and overwhelmed and will understandably prioritize themselves.

Leg #3: Proactive Outbound Calling or Connecting

While proactive outbound calling isn't exactly the most enjoyable or the most efficient thing to do, it is the *only* thing you can control. Yes, it sounds like 2003 but what's the alternative? Waiting at your desk for marketing to feed you more leads? Waiting for your network to magically think of you and make introductions on your behalf?

You have a choice. You can be reactive and wait to be fed leads or you can be proactive, go on the offensive, and cast a wide net to strangers who don't know you from Adam. And in doing so, choose the only form of lead generation that will always be controllable and manageable. You can't control your marketing department. You can't control your referrals. But you *can* control the number of sales calls you or your team makes.

While I'm not advocating that proactive calling should be your first preferred method of filling your sales pipeline, what I am saying is that relying on inbound leads and referrals alone is an unbalanced effort. It is vitally important to supplement your sales pipeline by being proactive if you want to keep your job or you want your business to succeed.

And if you are still uncertain as to whether or not you need help with connecting, be brutally honest and ask yourself:

- **Is your phone ringing off the hook with hot prospects contacting you first?**

- **Is your marketing department flooding you with inbound leads?**

- **Is your sales team overwhelmed with referrals and introductions from your collective networking efforts?**

Provided you answered "no" to even one of these questions, prospecting must be part of your long-term sales strategy. If I have learned anything over the years, it's this: *there aren't enough inbound leads or referrals to sufficiently fill the top of the sales funnel.* It doesn't matter if your company has an amazing marketing department or if you are a disciplined networker. Prospecting is not an option. Instead, it is the lifeblood of your pipeline.

Take the time to examine the three legs of your lead generating stool. If the first two legs aren't producing enough leads to hit your quota or keep your sales pipeline full, you must supplement your efforts with sales connecting. And while this book isn't about how to generate more inbound leads or how to get more referrals or introductions from your existing network, it is about how to effectively and efficiently prospect to create balance for the times when inbound leads and networking simply aren't enough. Just as the game of baseball requires a balance of skill, effort, and art, filling your pipeline demands the same.

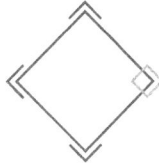

CHAPTER 1:
It's All About Connecting

"Hardship often prepares an ordinary person for an extraordinary destiny."
– C.S. Lewis

I was born in Saigon, Vietnam in 1973. Left on the steps of an orphanage at the end of the war, I along with two other boys were discovered wrapped in newspaper. I was the only one to survive. And while many might find this beginning a sad one, it opened the door to something good.

As an extension of World Vision, a relief organization and international adoption agency, the orphanage sought to match children with families in other countries who were unable to have their own. Although my parents had long dreamed of having a large family, they quickly realized they would only be able to have two biological children. World Vision became their way forward in growing their family through adoption.

Like me, both of my parents came from seemingly hard beginnings. My dad grew up with an absent mother and an alcoholic father (who would later commit suicide.) And my mom grew up in foster care, never knowing her own family. But for both of them, it sparked a desire to adopt, which not only led to my adoption but also the subsequent adoption of 8 more siblings.

Growing up, life was exceptionally normal. I had two loving parents and a tight-knit family who ate dinner together at least 6 nights a week. My dad was a plumber/pipefitter by trade and my mom, a homemaker. And while I spent most of my childhood and teen years near Topeka, Kansas, the years following my adoption included several moves—from California to Texas to Oklahoma before finally settling in Silver Lake, Kansas.

Found just seven miles northwest of Topeka, Silver Lake boasts a population of only 1,439 and to this day has no traffic lights. Everyone knows everyone else. And while I attended kindergarten through high school in Silver Lake, I struggled to find it interesting. Resources were limited and with only 52 in my graduating class, the pond was small. Looking back, however, it was during this period that the entrepreneurial bug bit. From doing fellow students' homework for a fee to going door-to-door for school fundraisers, I loved finding monetary value in time well-spent.

Following high school, I attended Washburn University. (Go Ichabods!) And while I had intended to stay at Washburn for only two years and then transfer to The University of Kansas, I loved the advantages of having a smaller student population. Ultimately, I decided to remain at Washburn. I spent my first two years as an accounting major because I'd heard that CPA's make a considerable amount of money. But when I landed in Intermediate Financial Accounting, the class that separates the curious from the serious, and received a 37% on my first test *after* the curve, I promptly left accounting behind to pursue my Bachelor's Degree in both Marketing and Management.

To pay my way through college, I was the student cliche. I waited tables. I did odd jobs. I applied for paid internships. And I even landed a job at a call center named Pro-Tel Marketing. Its setup consisted of a large room with people elbow to elbow doing old school telemarketing. Even during training, turnover was constant. I remember that following a bathroom break, I noticed that another trainee had yet to come back. Concerned that he might be sick, I told my trainer who subsequently laughed at me with an evil grin and said, "He ain't coming back!"

Even though I only made $7 an hour and turnover was extremely high, this job gave me my first real taste of sales. Calling on behalf of major credit card companies, we would offer auto or dining plans using an automatic dialer. Moreover, we were required to read our scripts and objections verbatim as going off script was grounds for termination. While I enjoyed the work and won several "Rep of the Month" awards, one day I found myself bored with its monotony and decided to goof off by shooting rubber bands in the air. Unfortunately for me, I ended up hitting my supervisor in the eye and was fired on the spot.

Not long after I parted ways with Pro-Tel, a classmate of mine helped me secure an internship at American Express Financial Advisors. As part of working for three financial advisors, I would reach out to senior citizens and invite them to lunch seminars in an attempt to convert them into clients. In addition to inviting them to these monthly luncheons, I would also follow up with those who were unable to attend and invite them to future events. At this time, both email and the internet were still fairly new so the primary source of communication and connection was via phone.

While I considered both law school and pursuing an MBA after graduation, a chance conversation led me to jump directly into the workforce and find employment in Washington, D.C. From 1998 to 2000, I worked for a non-profit, telecom, and public relations firm and it was an absolute blast. Not only did I get to frequently chat with famous and well-known folks that we all know from the nightly news, but I was also responsible for securing interviews with these same folks on behalf of my clients. What was my main form of contact? The phone of course. I used it daily to reach out on my client's behalf, make introductions, schedule interviews, and conduct post-interview follow-up. It was a constant exercise of learning how to use the phone effectively to make connections.

In August of 2000, I moved to the Kansas City metro to be closer to my family. With it being only an hour away from home, living in Kansas City allowed me to maintain independence but still be close enough to those I loved. While I had mixed feelings about leaving DC, I was also grateful for the experience and the opportunity to bring that experience to my future professional endeavors. But like most recent college graduates, I had quite a bit of consumer debt. Having racked up $23,000 on credit cards, $7,000 from my car loan, and another $10,000 in student loans, my credit score had fallen to 513 and I had creditors calling me daily. It was humiliating! On top of that, the job I had (and hated) was only paying me $31,000 a year.

To say I was desperate was an understatement.

Then I did something most would label unconventional. I took a 100% commissioned sales job. The opportunity arose when the owner of a small but growing home improvement business reached out to me. He informed me that he was hiring because it was growing quickly. So much so that he had already begun opening branches across the country. Not only was I grateful for the opportunity, but I was also extremely fortunate that the sales manager took me under his wing, invested in me, and taught me how to sell. The formula was as simple as it was motivating: If you don't sell, you don't get paid. Not only did I nearly double my salary in the three years working with him, but I also made a major step forward in getting out of debt. In large part, because I found myself inspired by financial guru Dave Ramsey and his book, ***The Total Money Makeover: A Proven Plan for Financial Fitness.*** All of these things along with being solely reliant on commissions allowed me to truly learn the art of sales and connection.

In 2004, I met Kate, my future wife. A month before we were married, I moved from that 100% commission based sales position to a corporate sales job with normal daytime hours. In large part, the move was intended to give my wife and me the margin to see each other regularly and focus on building our life together. As a result, I became the Director of Sales for a small software company in Lenexa, Kansas. We demonstrated and sold management and accounting software and training to plumbers, electricians, and general contractors nationwide. Nearly 99% of business sales were acquired through the phone and Internet, which was challenging in and of itself. Even though I helped grow the company's revenue by 156%, I ultimately found myself at odds with my boss and we decided to part ways.

Shortly following my departure, a former boss asked me if I had ever considered starting my own company. I answered with a quick and emphatic, "No." But then he shared a story with me about another friend who had gone out on his own and built a successful lead generation company in South Carolina. Following a few interviews and an offer that I ended up declining, my wife and I soon realized that venturing out on my own was possible. We had no debt (except for our mortgage.) We had no children. And we knew the timing couldn't get any better. In the end, it was my wife who determined, "It's either now or never!"

It seemed that life had finally opened the door for me to combine my love of bringing people together with my ability to forge successful business relationships. Out of that opportunity, my business partner and I started a lead generation company. He owned 51% and I owned 49%. As in all things, whoever owns that extra percent calls the shots. We worked together from 2006 to 2010 before parting ways amicably.

In March 2010, Connect 5000, a Kansas City-based lead generation, prospecting training, and sales consulting firm, was born. Naming my company came rather easily. "Connecting" is the heart of what we do and "5000" represents the Fortune 5000 nearly all companies are trying to woo. Over the years, we have developed a specialty in connecting Fortune 5000 decision-makers with technology and consulting companies who maintain high average sales. In other words, companies hire us to "connect" and "prospect" potential buyers for their service or product. We make the introduction and get out of the way. Simply put, connecting is not only what we do but also who we are.

And while the very thought of connecting (aka prospecting,) often makes those in sales cringe, it is vital to consistent sales success. Too often prospecting gets pushed to the bottom of the to-do list because it's mundane and tedious. As a result, most aren't very skilled at doing it once it does become a priority. Opening the door is the challenge. But once inside it, a certain percentage will eventually become deals. This is how we've been able to multiply sales by making call after call after call on our clients' behalf. We schedule sales meetings with Fortune 5000 decision-makers and all the client has to do is show up and do what they do best—sell.

For over a decade, Connect 5000 has made meaningful introductions that lead to profitable connections. And during this tenure, I have learned how to equip and empower my clients to become skilled connectors in their own right. This book is your opportunity to gain that knowledge for yourself. It serves to aid any person working in technology or consulting who has to prospect on their own and any small business owner who sells professional services with high average sales and no marketing department. In every chapter, you will be given the rules of the game in a clear, actionable framework and a process that will increase your profitability.

SCOREBOARD SUMMARY:

Because sales are all about revenue, the only way to generate it consistently is through outbound connections. Simply put, inbound leads and referrals typically are not enough to solidly fill your pipeline. You must supplement your efforts by proactively and purposefully reaching out to prospects consistently.

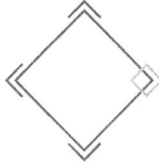

CHAPTER 2:
Breaking the Noise Barrier

"One person's data is another person's noise." – K.C. Cole

The current sales landscape is littered with obstacles, noise, and challenges. Throw in additional outside forces like the 2020 worldwide pandemic and it gets even noisier. But no matter the obstacle or challenge, we must first consider what prevents us from catching a prospect's attention and moving us closer to home plate. In communication, this kind of barrier is referred to as cognitive dissonance. But for our purposes, we will refer to it as five-fold: noise, decision fatigue, ad bombardment, attention spans, and email inbox overload.

Noise

Noise is everywhere. From Facebook to Twitter to Instagram, social media vies for our time, attention, and engagement. This is made even more obvious when we examine social media numbers, numbers that will only continue to grow with time. By the first quarter of 2020, Facebook reported having 2.6 billion monthly active users.[2] As of 2019, LinkedIn had over 660 million users;[3] Twitter had 330 million users;[4] and Pinterest, 335 million users.[5] It's incredible to consider that these numbers don't even include other social media giants, like Snapchat and Instagram.

But beyond social media noise is the influx and overabundance of blogs, due in large part to "experts" identifying them years ago as the next and newest way to increase sales and bring in warm leads. As of 2019, an overwhelming 600 million blogs existed.[6] Then the tides changed and content marketing took blogging's place even though it was essentially blogging with a new name.

Mark Schaefer of www.businessesgrow.com, spoke to the explosion of on-line content this way: *"Of course, the volume of free content is exploding at a ridiculous rate. Depending on what study you read, the amount of available web-based content (the supply) is doubling every 9 to 24 months."*[7] Schaefer goes on to say that companies with the deepest pockets (Amazon, Apple, Facebook, etc.) will inevitably win people's attention in the long run. Combine that with the additional noise of personal and professional email inboxes, the current content overload is causing attention spans to become shorter and shorter, which is why even I am blogging less and less.

Decision Fatigue

Decision fatigue has become a way of life. Various internet resources estimate that we make approximately 35,000 decisions in a single day.[8] Let me repeat that--we face up to 35,000 decisions *per day.* That in and of itself makes our job as connectors all the more challenging. While a good number of these decisions are automatic and don't require much thought, countless other decisions demand and consume both our mental and emotional energy. If we don't capture someone's attention quickly, people default to the status quo as it is easier to do nothing than to make a decision.

Ad Bombardment

Ad bombardment is yet another barrier to capturing our already overwhelmed attention spans. With more media channels comes more advertising. It is estimated that we are exposed to approximately 4,000 to 10,000 advertisements a day.[9] Even on the low end, these numbers are still impressive especially when combined with the numbers assigned to other barriers.

Attention Spans

Short attention spans create our next barrier. Microsoft did a study several years ago that found that in 2000, the average attention span was 12 seconds. But today, that average is only 8 seconds. Ironically, goldfish have an attention span of 9 seconds.[10] This essentially means goldfish have longer attention spans than humans do, which only reinforces why we must prioritize concise and clear language when connecting with potential clients.

Email Inbox Overload

The dreaded email inbox is the final barrier to sales connection. All you have to do is take a moment to examine the number of unread emails in your work and personal inboxes to know this kind of noise is real and overwhelming. The McKinsey Global Institute found that an average employee spends 13 hours a week reading and responding to email, which accounts for approximately 28% of his/her workweek.[11] According to Radicati's Email Report, there were 2.6B email users in 2015. By the end of 2019, there were 2.9B users.

The real problem for those of us in sales is there is too much noise and content available. In many ways, it is much easier for those we are targeting to ignore us rather than to engage with us. And while it may go without saying, this also applies to already overwhelmed executives whose time is scarce and valuable.

While we need to identify professional barriers to connection, we also need to consider that personal barriers exist as well. Not too long after we were married, my wife and I agreed that we wouldn't start a family or get any pets as we transitioned to being newlyweds. A year later, my wife said she wanted a baby. I answered, "Let's get a dog." A few weeks later, we would bring a 6-week-old Labrador Retriever home. For nearly thirteen years, Zoey was a wonderful dog and a loyal companion. But following surgery to remove a malignant mass, she deteriorated quickly and we had to make the difficult but humane decision to end her pain.

What's the sales lesson here?

When we communicate with clients or prospects by phone, email, or in person, you never truly know what's going on in their personal or professional lives. We all can put on a brave face in the middle of overwhelming circumstances. But know if prospects seem down, distracted, or impersonal, there may be things going on in their lives that you may not be able to see but that will affect their ability to hear you. Even though I would consider myself an extrovert, I remained fairly stoic and quiet in the days following our goodbye to Zoey. And even when I tried to put on a brave face, I know it affected my interactions with others and my ability to listen to them. It will serve you well to be aware that your prospects and clients can and will experience the same.

Noise + Decision Fatigue + Ad Bombardment + Short Attention Spans + Social Media + Email Inbox Overload = Very Overwhelmed Prospect or Executive

SCOREBOARD SUMMARY:

No matter what barrier you find yourself up against, remember that content consumption will always have a limit. By being both proactive and personal, you can give yourself the best chance at making a connection despite the noise. Just keep in mind that rejection is part of the game so accept it, move on, and keep doing the things you can control.

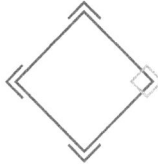

CHAPTER 3:
The Discipline of Consistency

*"In a perfect world, you and I probably wouldn't exist,
so let's not hope for one."* – Ze Frank

I am a lifelong Kansas Jayhawk fan. And like any good Jayhawk, two things are permanently etched in my memory--their title win in 1988 and their repeat win in 2008. On the outside, it may not seem impressive to win only 2 titles in 27 years. But the Hawks make up for it in holding the longest-running streak of NCAA appearances, demonstrating their program's consistent commitment to excellence.

In contrast, one of KU's biggest rivals, the Kentucky Wildcats, holds an impressive 8 National Titles. While there is no denying the success of their program or the stellar coaching by John Calipari, there have been years where the Cats have not even made the postseason tournament. But what does this have to do with sales? In a word, consistency.

Take a moment to weigh in on the consistency of your sales reps. Do they faithfully hit their numbers or are they inconsistent with some great wins along the way? Now ask yourself, "Would I rather have a sales team that consistently hits their numbers year in and year out or a team that's irregular and unpredictable but lands some very big clients every once in a while?"

While big wins feel good, consistent success over a significant period will not only heighten a company's credibility but it will also sustain long-term growth. In a perfect world, we would possess an overflowing pipeline, a marketing department that provides more leads than we can handle, and a network that requires little to no outbound calls. But folks, that's just not realistic. Although there is always a minuscule chance to land a dream client on the first attempt at connection, the reality is we will all find ourselves at a point where we need to supplement our pipelines in a consistent and somewhat predictable way.

Based on research from Rain Today, 50% of salespeople won't prospect. Even worse, the percentage of consultants who won't prospect is even higher. Insidesales.com observed it takes 6 to 8 attempts to reach a decision-maker. Their research showed most sales reps only make 1.7 attempts before giving up. So, if you're trying to reach C-level executives, expect to make at least 12 to 14 attempts.[12]

But here's the good news: After studying 4,658 actual business technology buyers, Marketing Sherpa found that more than 50% admitted to short-listing a vendor after receiving a well-timed and relevant phone call.[13] DiscoverOrg found that 60% of IT executives say an outbound call or email led to a technology vendor being evaluated. Also, 75% took it a step further, attending an event or taking an appointment as a result of a cold call or email.[14]

In the past, I could make 100 sales calls and consistently set up 4 to 5 meetings. But unfortunately, those days are over. Most executives don't have desk phones and largely prefer to use their cell phones as their work phones. Unless you have a prospect's cell phone or direct office number, you'll have to become more resourceful in looking for the needle in the proverbial haystack.

Moreover, it is naive to assume that your prospect will respond quickly. Getting them to respond is on us as the connectors. Now do prospects sometimes respond on the first try? Absolutely. That's where timing and luck come into play. But those are also factors you can't control. Learn to expect a 90% plus no response rate, whether it's utilizing the telephone, email, snail mail, or LinkedIn.

Just like a baseball team needs people whose skill set is suited to the appropriate positions, there are two roles needed on a sales team to strengthen a pipeline: the sales hunter and sales farmer. Sales Hunters open doors with new prospects and accounts, convert them into clients, and move on to new business. Sales Farmers deepen the existing relationship with the client by doing everything to make the client satisfied and maintain, expand, and cross-sell the account. The truth is you need both hunters and farmers in sales. And if you work for a small company, you will typically need to be comfortable being both in the beginning. But as you and your business grow, it will become more and more important to identify the strengths and weaknesses of you and your team so you can assign tasks accordingly.

If a rep is great at prospecting and setting up meetings but not so great at closing deals, that person might be more ideally suited for an inside sales role. If a rep is not good at opening doors, approaching potential clients and/or getting meetings with key decision-makers but is solid at converting prospects into clients, he or she might be best suited to be an outside sales representative. Keep in mind that just because someone doesn't excel in one area of sales doesn't mean they aren't suited to the job as a whole.

Consider Michael Jordan, who is arguably considered the best basketball player ever to play the game. 6-time NBA Champion. 5-time NBA MVP. 14-time NBA All-Star. But what many forget is that Jordan tried to be a professional baseball player as well. And to put it nicely, he was anything but successful.

Now does this ill-fated attempt diminish Jordan's basketball accomplishments? Absolutely not. Even though he wasn't overwhelmingly successful at baseball, his gift set was simply more well suited for basketball.

Was his legacy tainted? I doubt it. He was and is a great athlete. So in the same way, take the time to reflect on your strengths and of those on your team. Who among your team are the hunters? The farmers? A combo of both? And is there someone not excelling because they're in the wrong "sport"?

Once you begin to evaluate your team's strengths and weaknesses, you should purposefully consider where they belong and encourage them to do the things that in the long-term will make them successful. Yes, we live in a society of instant gratification. Yes, we want immediate results. Yes, we rarely want to wait for what is best in the long haul. But remember Slim Fast? The name itself points to quick weight loss. But is it healthy to lose a lot of weight in a very short amount of time? Or are we better off exercising more, eating healthier, and letting the numbers gradually decline? We all know the answer. Healthy bodies need healthy habits. The same proves true for sales.

Decide whether you want to be a "Jayhawk" or a "Wildcat." Do you want to be steady and consistent? Or do you want to be a roller coaster of inconsistency? While your sports loyalties might lie elsewhere, the best sales answer will forever and always be, "A Jayhawk."

SCOREBOARD SUMMARY:

Be diligent about identifying your strengths and weaknesses. Use those to determine what "sport" fits your skillset and talents. Then work diligently to prioritize healthy work and sales habits over instant gratification. Because no matter how booming the sales economy appears, slow, steady, and consistent always wins. Just as panicked, desperate, and inconsistent will always fail.

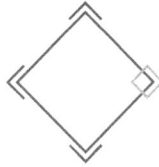

CHAPTER 4:
You Can't Sell Steak to Vegetarians

"The only thing that holds you back from getting what you want is paying attention to what you don't want." – Abraham Hicks

I have a confession.

I am bald *by choice.* I began shaving my head in 2000 and I've never looked back. To maintain the look, I visit our local Great Clips every 10 to 12 days. Predictably, my bill ends up being anywhere between $5 – $14, depending on whether or not I have a coupon. Not only is the price affordable, but my hairdresser is also a consummate professional and always does excellent work. Directly following a visit, I will typically go home and shower, a habit made easier as I only live two miles away. Clearly, I am the kind of customer Great Clips targets.

Until recently, I had never gone anywhere else. But then I received a coupon for a complimentary haircut in the mail and decided to use it. When I arrived for my appointment, I checked in at the front desk. Whereupon the person behind the desk offered me something to drink, took my jacket, put it in a locker, and handed me the key. As I walked back to the hairdresser's station, I noticed a pool table, spa rooms, locker rooms, and a members-only bar. Not only did I get my head shaved, but it was also massaged, rinsed, and washed, complete with hot towel service. The average price depending on what package you ordered was between $50-$100. The experience was top notch and it catered to a high-end clientele.

But aside from my grooming habits, what can we learn from this story?

Simply put, getting to first base requires that you clearly articulate your target audience. Not only does it help you, but it also helps potential prospects and clients as well. You wouldn't try to sell steak to vegetarians or hire a foot specialist to perform eye surgery. In the same way, it doesn't matter how good of a salesperson you are if you target the wrong audience.

But if you find yourself uncertain as to who your target audience is, begin by taking a moment to write down your top past and present clients on a sheet of paper or in a spreadsheet. Determine similarities so you know what they have in common and then use those similarities as building blocks for defining your target audience. Then ask yourself the following questions:

"Who does my sales organization cater to?"

"Who's our ideal client?"

"Does our target audience include everyone or is it more specialized?"

"Is our product or service targeted to the masses like *Great Clips*? Or do we have someone specific in mind with a certain income level, profession, geography, or type of business?"

The key is to be very clear as to who you can help. For example, if a lawyer were to identify himself by saying, "I am a generalist," people may or may not hire him. But if he/she was to take it one step further and say, "I am a divorce lawyer." That would narrow the scope and define his/her target audience. If one were to want to go even further in a niche, he/she might say, "I am a divorce lawyer for people over 50."

When it comes to defining your target audience, you need to have a ruthlessly clear understanding of who you've helped in the past, who your most successful clients are, and then go after companies similar to them. To be successful in any type of marketing campaign, you should be able to articulate an ideal target company's characteristics and decision-makers, as well as the pain, problem, or challenge you are uniquely able to solve.

For example, Connect 5000's dream clients meet the following criteria:

1. Our ideal clients are software, technology, and consulting companies with high average sales with annual revenue typically between $5M - $500M.

2. Within an organization, the right executive decision-maker may be one of the following: Chief Executive Officer, President, Vice President of Marketing, Revenue, Sales, Sales Operations, or Demand Generation.

3. The company ideally doesn't have an effective outbound sales prospecting strategy in place. Or the sales team struggles connecting with decision-makers. Or lead generation or sales prospecting training is a current challenge or priority. Or they are short-handed on inside business development reps and look to us to supplement their efforts.

Another tactic for identifying your ideal customer is to consider successful marketing campaigns of brand names. What does Lexus sell? If you said automobiles, you're technically correct. But what they really sell is status and luxury. How about ADT? Yes, they sell alarm systems. But what they offer their customers is peace of mind and security.

Now take the time to think about your product or service. What is the technically correct answer? And what results or outcomes do you sell instead? What are clients truly buying from you?

Knowing the answers to these questions will help you to better understand who you are selling to and what will reach your intended audience most effectively. Getting this part right upfront helps with prospecting and connecting in the future. At Connect 5000, we solve top of the funnel challenges and sell shortened sales cycles and multiplied revenue.

Another key to having a well-defined target audience is composing an intentional and considered value proposition. If you are finding it difficult to write a value proposition, here's a simple fill-in-the-blank exercise that will give you a foundation on which to build it:

I/my company helps _____ companies who have challenges with _____, resulting in _____.

Even with this template, it's completely normal to go through several revisions before you find the right value proposition. Once you identify your value proposition, write down your ideal company profile, and ideal decision-maker within the organization. Consider those answers in light of your value proposition. (**What pain, problems and challenges do you solve?**) And ultimately work diligently to focus on outcomes, not methods.

Just as it is important to identify who your target audience is, it is equally important to attend events and go places where your target decision-makers go. Case in point: Not long ago I attended a networking event for a non-profit here in Kansas City after they asked me to consider serving on their board of directors. It was pleasant and I had a good time. While in attendance, someone asked me if I often attended events like these. And I told him no and explained that CEO's and Sales VP's of companies that I want to do business with typically don't attend these events. Instead, I attend events that include attendees who are in our target niche-- like Oracle Open World, Microsoft's Worldwide Partner Conference, SXSW in Austin, etc.

Willie Sutton famously said he robbed banks because that's where the money was. It's the same with networking events. Go to places your target audience attend. And remember that executive decision-makers don't normally hang out at your local Chamber of Commerce.

If you are in the beginning stages of your business and you don't have a clear picture as to who the decision-makers are when sales connecting, reach out to the CEO and talk to his/her executive assistant and ask them a simple question that goes along the lines of, "Who reports to your CEO that's responsible for decisions regarding <blank>?" "Or who reports to your CEO that heads up such and such?"

In some manner, the executive assistant will give you one of three responses:

1. "I don't know." (Depending on the size of the firm, he/she literally may not know.)
2. "Go away." (Company policy may forbid them from giving out names and titles.)
3. "You need to talk to so and so." (A busy gatekeeper wants to get you off the phone quickly and back to what he or she was doing. Bam! You now have a quasi-warm introduction.)

If at this point, you are still unsure as to who your target decision-maker is, take a look at your past sales and clients and ask yourself, "In work with previous organizations, where did I start the relationship or conversation that got things rolling?" What common titles do they hold? Was it the VP of Finance? Was it the head of sales? Was it the Director of IT?" Start asking yourself these questions and go after a more like-minded audience.

Nicholas Read and Stephen Bistritz discuss how to identify the relevant executive in their book *Selling to the C-Suite*:

"It could be someone who has great influence with very little formal rank."

Ask 2 questions: Who will really evaluate, decide, or approve the decision?

AND

Who has the highest rank and greatest influence?[15]

Yes, titles are important and lots of people think they need to start with the CEO to start the sales cycle. There's some truth to that but it depends on the size of the company.

For example, if a company employs 50 people, the CEO may be the decision-maker. Maybe not. Titles are misleading. There are people with titles of "Vice President" who have very little decision-making power. Banks are notorious for giving out Vice President titles but without any actual decision-making authority. Depending on the size of the company, one Vice President might be on the same level as a Director at another firm.

Page 74 sums Read and Bistritz's point best: *"Another way to determine the relevant executive is to find the highest-ranking executive who stands to gain the most or lose the most as a result of the project or application associated with the sales opportunity."*[16]

The CEO of a company is very similar to the President of the United States. Ultimately in charge of everyone and everything but cannot handle every aspect of the business. There aren't enough hours in the day. Yes, the President is responsible for the military but most of the decisions are made by the Secretary of Defense, the Joint Chiefs of Staff, etc. If you get the CEO live, it is always worth the ask to try and get a meeting with him. He may direct you to the person responsible and as such, you now have a referral or introduction to get to the next base--a meeting with the relevant executive.

SCOREBOARD SUMMARY:

In sales, half the battle is getting in the door and the other half is staying there. Become a specialist, know your niche, and be targeted in your approach. Because ultimately, success only comes to those who target well.

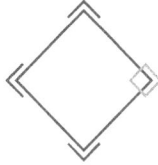

CHAPTER 5:
Train Like a Champion

"Change is the only constant in life." – Heraclitus

Nothing says fun like an expired license and a day at the DMV. So when it came time for me to most recently renew, I was determined to be at the head of the line. I left my house at 6:45 a.m. and arrived at 6:49 a.m. But when I pulled into the parking lot, I discovered that four other people had come with the same purpose in mind. Noticing that none of them had chosen to get out of their respective cars, I decided to brave the cold and the wind by walking to the main entrance, subsequently becoming the first person in line. A few minutes later, those still in their cars followed suit. By the time the doors opened at 7 a.m., 13 people were standing in line, and being the first, I was in and out in all of 7 minutes.

Translated into sales language, this story demonstrates that it's not enough to just show up. You also have to play the game well. 4 people arrived before I did, but I was the first to take action and create a line that would translate into being the first one served.

When making sales prospecting calls each day, the same holds. You have to do more than show up. You have to make the time to pick up the phone and reach out to potential prospects. It's simply not enough to plan to do it or want to do it. You have to pick up the phone and dial out.

Ultimately, I get it. We all are busy and overwhelmed. No one has the time to make connecting calls. But the reality is we have to make the time. As Gordon MacDonald eloquently said: "Seize your time before it seizes you!" Or in the words of Mike Weinberg, "No one defaults to prospecting mode. New business development doesn't just happen. We must carve out time to do it. It's seldom urgent, although it is highly important."

When you signed up for a sales position, you signed up to prospect and connect. When you agreed to take a salary, you agreed to the strings attached to it. And whether you like it or not, one of those strings requires constantly hunting for new business. Non-sales employees and colleagues are counting on you to continually fill the top of the sales funnel and your success or failure is also key to staying in business and keeping the doors open.

Even though this may seem reason enough, you still might doubt the importance of prospecting if you are new to the business or have always maintained a healthy pipeline. But even while the status quo may seem to be working, there are other important reasons to stay active in your prospecting and connecting efforts.

Reason Number 1: Companies get acquired.

If you read the newspapers or watch the news, companies are acquired quite regularly. It happens in both good and bad economies. It's even happened a few times at Connect 5000. The best example that comes to mind is the connection we fostered with Vela Systems.

Vela Systems' Vice President of Sales, Gary Greenberger, hired us to connect them with the top 400 largest construction firms nationwide. Through targeted email and sales prospecting campaigns, we were able to provide Vela with over 120 introductory meetings with project executives in 6 months. Why did we stop? Vela Systems was acquired by Autodesk and our agreement ended. The acquiring company didn't have an agreement with us and brought operations in-house. But our experience was not limited to Vela Systems. Talari was a client for 22 months before Oracle acquired them. And Hedvig worked with us 10 months before Commvault bought them out. So rather than being surprised when acquisition happens, expect that it will.

Reason Number 2: Companies go out of business every single day.

Do you remember Lehman Brothers from the early 2000s? Lehman was the fourth-largest U.S. investment bank at the time of its collapse boasting 25,000 employees worldwide. If they can disappear overnight, so can your clients. Their demise may be expected or an absolute surprise. But either way, if one client makes up an overwhelming percentage of your business, be mindful to go after other clients and decrease that percentage. Diversify your client portfolio just as you do with your retirement.

Reason Number 3: Companies undergo executive leadership changes.

Far too often, the executive contact who hired your firm resigns or is terminated. And unfortunately, the new CEO doesn't have a relationship with you or in some cases, even knowledge of you. Moreover, he/she may bring in his or her team of people. Is it fair? Nope. Is it life? Absolutely. You never know when a client will leave you. It's one thing to lose a client because you underperformed. It's quite another when you lose a client due to external factors beyond your control.

Reason Number 4: Maintaining contact with previous clients can help to offset acquisitions and turnover.

Contacts can leave during both the pre-sales and post-sales phases with existing clients. At Connect 5000, we've experienced both. In a good economy, it seems that 20% of the workforce changes positions. In bad economies, layoffs and restructurings happen daily (Covid-19 anyone?) I once had a client who was the Chief Sales Officer at an outsourcing firm based in New York City. We met in person, communicated regularly, and she was pleased with our efforts. But then she gave a month's notice to the firm that she was pursuing other opportunities. Our relationship was then transferred to the Vice President of Marketing. In many ways, we became a red-headed stepchild in that we added responsibility to her already overflowing plate. Our agreement ended shortly and abruptly. It served as a brutal but effective reminder as to why it is important to always keep your pipeline full.

But it is also important to note that a change in leadership can also work in your favor. Gary Greenberger, who I mentioned above, stayed in touch with me over the years. After Vela Systems was acquired, he went on to work for a biotech firm. Guess who he called? Connect 5000. He placed so much value on what we had done in the past that even through an acquisition and job change, we were the first company he called and our engagement lasted 17 months.

Another example in our favor included one of my LinkedIn connections who is a Chief Marketing Officer in the San Francisco Bay area. He hired us for the first time a few years ago and then his company was acquired. When he moved on to another firm, he reached out again and he was our client for 22 months until Oracle acquired his company. Not long after the acquisition, he hired us for the 3rd time at his new firm. Moral of the story? Stay in contact with your connections and if you do excellent work, they will hire you again.

Reason Number 5: Your existing contact leaves the company during the sales cycle.

Not only can a change in leadership affect your existing client base, but it can also affect the sales process before a company becomes a client. You may do the hard work, find an ideal company, engage, qualify the prospect that has pain and problems that your firm can fix. But right about the time, you're ready to count the revenue and cash your commission check, boom! You call your contact and that person is no longer with the firm and you have to start all over again. If you've been in sales for some time, this has most likely already happened to you.

For example, I had a discovery call with a Lexmark marketing executive. We were not a fit at that time, so she requested I contact her several months later. I immediately sent her a calendar invite and she accepted it. But when I called her months later, she was no longer there. Lexmark had been acquired and she had moved on.

While I ruthlessly keep our CRM database clean and updated, I've noticed that about 18-22% of sales and marketing executives move, get fired, or resign every couple of years. We aren't talking about entry-level employees. We are talking about major decision-makers, which is why it can be extremely frustrating to do your best to advance the sale only to have your contact leave.

Reason Number 6: The X factor.

Even in good economic times, there are factors beyond your control. Another September 11th happens nationwide. A company's funding gets pulled. A company gets sued, throwing everything off-kilter. (Yes, that happens daily too.) An unknown financial curveball comes straight out of left field and no one saw it coming (i.e. a worldwide pandemic.)

Not terribly long ago, a fractional CFO unexpectedly reached out to me. He was a consultant for another client of mine and listened in on calls, knew our track record and results, etc. We had multiple conversations with him as well as the CEO. If I were in Vegas, I would have bet highly that the odds were in our favor, particularly since he was a referral who had worked closely with one of my clients. (Referrals of that nature typically tend to move forward at a higher rate.)

After the CFO requested and received a proposal, he brought it to the board. But one of the board members put the brakes on the process because he had a local resource who specialized in calling on healthcare organizations. As a result, the prospect ended up going with them and informed me of the board's decision over the phone.

Examples like this demonstrate that even when something feels like a sure thing, it can always change. Just remember that a yes is better than no, a no is better than silence, and verbal deals are never a sure thing until the client signs a contract. Keep your sales pipeline full and always hunt for new business. You never know when a client may leave you or when that "sure" deal falls through due to circumstances beyond your control.

But keep in mind that there are also things within our control. We can commit to improving our sales and connecting skills every day. We can determine the number of sales calls we make and the number of emails we send. We can increase the number of times we try to connect with potential prospects.

Muhammed Ali once said, "I hated every minute of training but I said to myself, suffer now so you can live the rest of your life as a champion." Ali spent countless hours training, practicing, and improving his boxing skills for 15 rounds in the boxing ring. Hours upon hours versus 45 minutes in the ring, if it even lasted that long. How do Ali's words and practices apply to the sales world? Simply put, if we pay the price now, we'll enjoy sales success later.

SCOREBOARD SUMMARY:

Even though we live in a world of instant gratification, building a sales pipeline and relationships takes time and practice. It is vital to stay active and cultivate connections. Training like a champion now will ultimately ensure your ability to survive when circumstances change or clients leave in the future.

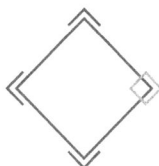

CHAPTER 6:
Mastering the Art of Credibility

*"Sales is a human business. Automation notwithstanding,
it is a business that is driven by relationships between humans."* – Andy Paul

On the 1st floor of my office building is a licensed counselor and therapist. In our limited interaction, I've found that he's a very nice guy. But not long ago, I ran into one of his former colleagues who works in the same building as well. In our conversation, I learned that even though my neighbor is a marriage and relationship counselor, he has been married and divorced twice.

As soon as I had that piece of information, I suddenly began to question his counseling chops. Am I making a snap judgment here? Of course, I am, if only to get my point across. While I have no insight as to why his two marriages didn't work out, my first thought was that if I had marital issues, I wouldn't go to this particular counselor.

Maybe it's unfair. Maybe I am passing judgment. Maybe I should be open to giving him a chance. But it points out our natural tendency to question someone's credibility. It is this same tendency that can affect prospective sales. When we interact with others, prospects are quick to judge, which can either serve us well or decimate our credibility.

As the old saying goes, you don't get a second chance to make a first impression. When we approach prospects, we need to remember prospective clients are constantly evaluating our level of credibility. Just as we also need to be actively aware of the things that affect our credibility and be willing to change them if we are wanting to make the most of our opportunity to secure a client. The reality is that most of these factors can be found in places outside our immediate sales world. Case in point? My recent selection to be on a jury for the very first time.

The civil trial involved a plaintiff suing the city and the police department for damages as a result of a car pursuit. While the baby survived, the plaintiff was suing for damages that sought to recover the lost wages of the deceased mother. Both the plaintiff and defendant presented their cases along with evidence and their theories of the case. After the trial, the judge dismissed us but instructed us to return the next day to deliberate. Before we could return, however, a settlement was reached.

While somewhat relieved that I did not have to be responsible for a verdict, I did note 5 things from the trial that translate into the sales world:

1. **Appearances matter.** You may not be able to control your looks, but you can control how you dress. When in doubt, dress up, and step up your wardrobe appropriately for the situation. While it may not be necessary for you to always wear a suit and tie or a dress, it is always advisable to dress with the situation in mind.

2. **Make eye contact when communicating with people.** The plaintiffs barely made eye contact with the jury. It could have been done intentionally or it could have been a simple case of nerves. On the flip side, the defense hardly looked at the person asking questions and looked at the jury instead, which was far more persuasive and effective.

3. **Be specific with numbers.** When an economics professor provided his analysis and estimation of lost wages, he was specific. He could have easily rounded up a number to say, $1,000,000. But

instead, he pointed to a specific figure of $983,753.00. And if for no other reason than this, it sounded more believable. When presenting pricing to prospective clients, this tactic can produce the same result and believability. When sharing with prospects as to how much you saved a client or helped generate some revenue figure, use specific, non-rounded numbers and it will naturally increase your credibility.

4. **Be prepared and thorough.** In this case, both the prosecution and defense met this requirement. When meeting with a client, do the same. Don't be sloppy or lazy and come prepared.

5. **Always strive to communicate well.** In the courtroom, whoever communicates the best usually wins. In essence, the plaintiff and defense were engaged in a sales contest. Money was involved and they were selling us on their side of the story. Thankfully, the jury didn't have to declare a winner or loser. But the experience demonstrated why it is important to communicate concisely, ask good questions, and use tools that will accomplish the task of connecting.

Not only is it imperative to build your credibility among clients, but it is also important to choose the right tools with which to make that connection. While there are countless tools out there that can be used for sales connecting and prospecting, it doesn't mean you should use them. You wouldn't use a sledgehammer to kill a gnat or a garden hose to water a wheat field. The same is true for sales.

As such, when it comes to casting a wide net, planting seeds, and making outbound calls to strangers, the key is to find the right tools that work for you. Consider the fundamental equipment (or tools) of baseball that have stood the test of time. Even with the evolution of the game and changes in technology, you still need a baseball, a bat, and a glove. In sales, the same idea applies. If you find yourself struggling to create a foundation, there are four fundamental tools I would recommend: the phone, email, LinkedIn, and snail-mail. These cost-effective tools *still* work no matter how much technology exists. Does anything work 100% of the time? Of course not. But used properly, they can make a big difference.

1. **Telephone**: Yes, I agree with you in advance. Executive prospects answer their phone less and less and ruthlessly screen out unfamiliar calls. But you can still use the phone to make mini-commercials or sound bites about your firm, differentiating yourself from the competition and allowing your personality and value proposition to shine.

2. **Email**. Not only popular but also free, email can cast a very wide net in a short amount of time. In fact, you can effectively and efficiently reach more people via email than you can by phone. Because email reaches prospects regardless of the time of day, you can effectively and efficiently reach more people via email than you can by phone.

3. **LinkedIn.** LinkedIn is the professional networking version of Facebook. While not every client originates from my LinkedIn connections, I find the majority of my business via LinkedIn. Using LinkedIn's filters, you can quickly build a targeted list and filter companies with certain criteria as well as find executives and other decision-maker titles. For the most part, a good majority of the 660 million users keep it to business rather than the emotional vomiting and political grandstanding you witness on Facebook. Hands down, it's one of the best tools to harness the power of connection.

4. **Snail Mail/Direct Mail:** For my young readers who are unsure of what snail mail is: it's a sales message with words typed up on a physical piece of paper or two with your name personally signed at the bottom, placed in an envelope and mailed through the

United States Postal Service. You can even include your business card inside the envelope. Sarcasm aside, direct mail still works. According to Neil Patel, with fewer marketers sending snail mail, your marketing piece has a higher chance of standing out.[17]

SCOREBOARD SUMMARY:

Establishing your credibility is key to communicating effectively. Always take the time to create content that speaks confidently. This, combined with the appropriate tools, will give you the greatest chance at a successful connection.

CHAPTER 6

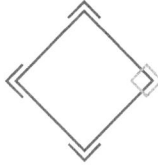

CHAPTER 7:
Harnessing the Power of Voicemail

"Those who say it can't be done shouldn't get in the way of those doing it." – Unknown

Even though some might argue this point, the phone is *still* an effective sales tool as long as you remember its unique role in prospecting and lead generation. Not only is the phone a more personal way to communicate with prospects, but it also allows you to see if you and the prospective client are a good fit during the sales process. The other advantage it provides is the ability to hear emotion even though you aren't face-to-face. When you use more impersonal communication like email, you might second guess what the prospect is saying and/or misunderstand what he/she is trying to convey.

Consider how many times you have received a response to an email and you aren't sure whether the person on the other end is mad, annoyed, or uninterested. Similar concerns may arise with text messaging. You send a text message to someone and he/she responds in all caps and you are left to wonder if the sender is angry. Just like when your mom learned to text for the first time, miscommunication can occur without understanding tone and context.

Picture a pop fly and a player on first. The crowd cheers thinking their team is one base closer to scoring. But then the ball is caught and the player is left to double back to first base. In the same way, other forms of connection can give you a false sense of security that your message has been received and connection has been made. Using the phone avoids this pitfall. Keep in mind that just because an email doesn't bounce back doesn't mean your prospect is still with the company. Information on LinkedIn and company websites are often neglected and outdated.

As with any communication, the key to effective prospecting by phone is having realistic expectations and remembering that a vast majority of your calls will go directly to voicemail. Simply put, people just don't answer their phones as often as they did in the past. So to be successful using it as a sales tool, you'll need to script several voicemails that are succinct, to the point, and pique curiosity. Remember, our attention span is only 8 seconds, so you have a small window in which to make a big impression. Another factor that requires a concise and effective script is the reality that most companies no longer have desk phones and most executives prefer to use their cell phones. The faster you can obtain a prospect's cell, the more successful you will be.

As you develop your script(s) and/or talk track, think of each voicemail as a mini-commercial. When Coca Cola creates a commercial, it doesn't air only once. It plays over and over again. In the same way, you have to do this with your voicemail messages, using a consistent talk track with only slight variations. Whether you are using the phone or voicemail, the number one goal is to pique interest. Keep in mind that while you may not talk to many people, the practice is necessary and will ultimately be worth your time.

At Connect 5000, we track campaign stats and have consistently found that you will get voicemail approximately 90 to 95% of the time. For companies who don't have work desk phones, your only option is to send an email. While we hope to connect live with about 10 people, the real goal is to convert 3 to 5 of those live people into appointments, meetings, discovery calls, demos, webinars, etc. In essence, you have a 95% failure ratio. This is consistent across various verticals, company revenue size, employee size, and geography.

In the business world, there's an endless debate on whether or not you should leave a voicemail or not. All too often, I'm asked, "Should I leave a message?" The answer is always "yes." If you're going through the trouble of calling someone, you might as well leave a message. Even if you have a 99% failure rate, you have a 1% chance of making a connection. If you don't leave a message, your chances drop to zero. Begin the process by sending an introductory email. Then follow up with a phone call and a voicemail that is scripted but sounds natural. Keep it brief and grab their attention.

A script that does both would look something like this: "Hi John, this is Ray Ruecker with Connect 5000. I'm following up on the email I sent recently. I noticed your LinkedIn profile and thought it might make sense to talk. Please call me back at 913-481-8941. Again, 913-481-8941."

The key is to prompt the prospect to ask himself/herself, "Who is Ray? Who is Connect 5000? What email is he referring to? Was the email important? I wonder how we're connected on LinkedIn?" It will be this curiosity that will drive them to their email and effectively earn you two touches. If you don't leave a message, not only will you run the risk of not connecting with the prospect, but you might be missing out on a potential sale or connection.

Not long ago, this nearly happened to my wife and me with our subscription to our satellite radio company. Unknowingly, I had let our subscription expire. For months, I kept getting a phone call from an 800 number that I just let go to voicemail. By the time I was curious enough to answer, the company had made at least 20 calls and never left a voicemail. But one day, curiosity got the better of me and I answered the phone. The person on the other end said, "Hey, we're your satellite radio provider and wanted to make sure you wanted to update your membership to avoid expiration." The first thing I said to him was, "I wish you would have left a voicemail from the get-go rather than make me wonder as to who was calling me."

When you don't leave a voicemail and you keep calling from the same number, it makes you look like a stalker, which typically makes people feel uncomfortable. The best and most effective practice is to leave a voicemail. Typically, I would recommend preparing up to 6-7 voicemails that provide a miniature commercial about who you are and what problems you solve for prospective clients. Keep in mind that if you do happen to catch someone live, always ask if it is a good time to chat. You never know if the prospect has answered the phone during a meeting, a doctor's appointment, or while going through security at the airport. No matter the situation, it always behooves you to show respect and professionalism.

When writing your scripts, begin with an opening statement that is short and well-rehearsed should someone answer the phone. It might go something along the lines of, "Hey, Bob, Ray Ruecker with Connect 5000. I am following up on an email I sent you this morning. Did I catch you in a meeting?" Notice that in each statement, I try to provide proper context as to why I am calling, I identify myself quickly, and then I conclude with professionalism and respect for their time.

While I have seen many scripts end with, "Is this a good or bad time to chat?" it is not my preference to do so. The problem with this particular question is that it is relative and the answer required is open-ended. By asking a question that requires a "yes" or "no," you give the prospect an easy and definitive parameter, which also allows you the benefit of using a scripted and/or planned response. No matter how you utilize the phone--be it as a follow-up or as an offensive sales strategy--we all want to know how many meetings we will generate. And the answer is...*it depends.*

Whenever I chat with sales candidates, I always ask them how many sales calls were required in their previous job. Their answer is nearly always 100 a day. The reality is that to achieve these numbers, you would have to make 1 call every 5 minutes (60 minutes divided by 12 calls per hour). If you are making 100 calls a day, you may not be having that many quality conversations. It's like a police officer who brags that he arrested 15 people last week. The true test of his success is in the number of convictions resulting from his arrests and it became an issue of quality over quantity.

Think of it in this way: When an airplane initially takes off, it requires a large amount of fuel. Similarly, when you're building a sales pipeline from scratch, you may have to make a large number of calls in a day to grow your book of business.

At Connect 5000, I expect my sales reps to make at least 50 to 60 calls per day. Keep in mind that calling the receptionist and asking who is the head of sales doesn't constitute a call. It is simply research. A call should only be counted when you talk to a decision-maker or leave them a voicemail message. With 50 – 60 calls per day adding up to 250 – 300 calls per week, it is safe to say that our representatives are making anywhere from 1000 – 1200 calls a month. Using our numbers at Connect 5000, the typical success ratio is 1 – 5%. That's it. Nothing sexy or glamorous. But 1000 – 1200 calls with a 1% success ratio will normally land 10 to 12 appointments per month and around 120 to 144 a year. The better a rep gets at prospecting, the less he or she has to do it as time goes by. This is due in large part to the fact that the more appointments he or she makes, the higher number of discussions, presentations, and proposals will come as a result.

It is also important to note while many sales reps avoid calling between Thanksgiving and the New Year under the assumption people are out on vacation, it is still a good time to connect because many companies are also planning and budgeting for the upcoming year. According to Rainsalestraining.com: "People with authority to make decisions in their organizations find money all the time for things that were not on their radar screens during business planning time, and so they can capitalize on opportunities as they arise."[18] Furthermore, according to Surveys by DemandGenReport: "... only 20% – 30% of purchases are budgeted at the beginning of the year. Between 70% and 80% of survey respondents say they evaluate potential solutions, build a business case for immediate adoption, and then obtain spending approval."[19]

In short, don't use the holiday season as a reason not to connect with potential clients. Constantly reach out to folks. Executives are always planning for both the existing and upcoming year. Your product or solution may not be on their radar until you connect with them. They don't know what they don't know. When in doubt, reach out to them. Remember the statistic from Art Sobczak? 50% of business technology buyers admitted to short-listing a vendor after receiving a well-timed and relevant phone call. So be bold, make the call, and don't rely on email marketing or social media alone.

As people often ask me for real-life samples to use when leaving voicemails for prospects, I have provided samples below. Keep in mind, however, that they are meant to build on one another. It is best to use them together and in order. Be prepared to constantly tweak, edit, and refine your voicemails until your message is clear and you've found your own voice.

1.   "Hello ____, Ray Ruecker with Connect 5000. I'm following up on an email I sent you recently. I noticed your LinkedIn profile and thought it might make sense to talk. Please call me back at ____. Again that number is ____."

2. "Hello _____, Ray Ruecker with Connect 5000. Most companies struggle with ____. I would love to share some solutions that have worked

really well for others in your industry. If this is of interest, let's set up a time to talk at _____. Again my number is _____."

3.   "Hello _____, Ray Ruecker with Connect 5000. I'm following up on an email I sent you recently. We generated a sales call for a client that resulted in a $27M contract. Please call me back at _____ and I'll share how we did it. Again my number is _____."

4.   "Hello _____, Ray Ruecker with Connect 5000. I'm following up on an email I sent you recently. We've generated over 120 meetings in 6 months for a company like yours. If you would like more meetings with new prospects, please call me back at _____. Again my phone number is _____."

5.   "Hello _____ Ray Ruecker with Connect 5000. I don't know if you're currently evaluating outbound lead generation firms, but if you are, I can offer you some insight that will help you make a better decision and only take 15 minutes of your time. If you are interested, please call me back at _____. Again my phone number is _____."

SCOREBOARD SUMMARY:

Success in any voicemail campaign requires a balance of time, effort, and touches. Even if prospects don't respond to your initial efforts, don't give up. Remember, it takes an average of at least 8 to 12 attempts to connect with a prospect. Throwing in the towel too early will often mean missed opportunities and lost profit.

CHAPTER 7

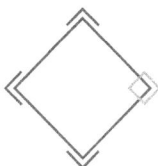

CHAPTER 8:
Standing Out in an Email Inbox

"Communication is not saying something; communication is being heard."
– Frances Hesselbein

Recently, I was referred to a Vice President of Sales for a technology company based in Iowa which also happens to have a local presence here in Kansas City. Even though I have several clients I've never met in person, this relationship was different. We chatted by phone. We met for lunch when he was in town. We exchanged emails regularly. But when I sent him a proposal, I misspelled his name. He noticed it immediately and when he pointed it out, he also asked if he should be concerned about my attention to detail. Ironically, I'm good at remembering names and spellings. But I blew it this time and I was left to apologize profusely and correct it. Thankfully, he still signed a contract.

Although it may seem obvious, two lessons learned here are:

1. Take extra time, proofread and double-check every email, proposal, and written form of communication that goes out.

2. When you make a mistake, apologize sincerely and immediately.

In this case, my client was gracious enough to point it out and not let my mistake kill the deal. But no matter how long we've been in sales, the little things can determine whether or not we stay stuck on first base or make it to home plate. While this applies to all written forms of communication, it is especially important when you are using email as your primary form of connection. In a recent national survey, Booher Research collaborated with the University of Northern Colorado's Social Research Lab. The survey revealed:

- 42% spend 3 or more hours per day reading and responding to email.

- 48% consider email their primary method of communication (more so than texting, phone, instant messaging, or face to face.)

- 55% check their email hourly or leave it open all the time.

- 24% expect a response to their email from "outside the organization" within an hour.[20]

With research confirming that email is one of the most popular forms of communication, it is vital to use it purposefully and intentionally in any sales campaign. According to ExactTarget, it takes less than four seconds for someone to decide whether he will read your email, delete it, forward it, or do something else with it, which is why brevity is an absolute must if you want to connect.[21] Keeping in mind that prospects have short attention spans and often require 8-12 attempts to connect, email should be your first line of communication.

Here are the reasons why:

1. You can cast a wide net and reach a large number of people in a short amount of time. Although the phone is important, you can only call a limited number of people per day.

2. People are more accessible electronically than by phone (think smartphones, tablets, etc.) In today's society, people work remotely and travel more frequently than in years past. Additionally, countless companies have simply done away with desk phones and employees use their cell phones as their work phone.

3. Typically, if a prospect is out of the office, they may have turned on an auto-responder. This automatically cues you into the prospect's availability. They may be out for work travel, paid time off, maternity leave, vacation, jury duty, etc.

4. Sending an email first can help identify if a viable prospect is no longer with the company. An email may come back non-deliverable or with a short note explaining that they left and whom to contact in the future with their contact information. This is particularly helpful when an executive doesn't update his/her LinkedIn profile regularly. Companies can be slow to remove an executive from their website as well.

5. The final advantage that an email gives you over other forms of communication is if an auto-response comes back, the prospect's direct phone number may be in the signature line. In the event your only contact information is an email, you now know his/her phone number as well with only one soft touch.

This also allows you to follow the sequence of communication I would recommend when you utilize both the telephone and email. Send the email first and then follow up with a phone call. Not only does it count as two touches, which meets the limit I recommend each week, it also gives you a solid reason to call your prospect. Even if you don't get a response from either attempt, wait a week and then try it again, following the same pattern of sending an email and then making a phone call as your means of following up. Just keep in mind that if the prospect responds or calls you back, the sequence changes and your response should be as soon as possible to maximize your chance of connecting and setting a meeting.

If the first email you send doesn't get a response, it simply may not resonate with the prospect. And that's okay. But when you send subsequent emails, share success stories and anecdotes on other offerings that have benefited your clients to pique their interest. Keep in mind that you are in it for the long haul. If you get a response on your first attempt, great! If you don't, keep at it and don't get frustrated. Some executives purposely don't respond to solicitations right away, no matter how enticing the email, telephone call, or offer. Why? They want to see if the rep is serious about connecting with them. By utilizing a multi-touch approach and coordinated attempts, you'll automatically build your credibility with your prospective clients.

Not sure if your emails are getting through to targeted prospects? A cost-effective tool that only costs around $12 to $25 a month is BananaTag. It will tell you when people open your email, with what device they opened the email, and the embedded links they clicked on, which is yet another check to see if your message is getting through to your prospect. There are countless services similar to BananaTag but it's the one I faithfully use at Connect 5000.

Now let's say you connect with a prospect and your contact goes dark, disappears, and doesn't return your call. Email is the perfect (and softest) way to revive a relationship/potential relationship, particularly if you adhere to the following guidelines:

1. Remember your goal. (Connect and get a meeting or discovery call. It's not to sell. Yet.)

2. Make it personal. (Use prospect's first name.)

3. Make it brief. (People have short attention spans.)

4. Make it suspenseful. (Pique interest and curiosity.)

Another element of an email that requires purpose and intention is the subject line. Typically, the most effective lines will be those that are vague, pique curiosity, and/or name drop. The following lines are some that we've successfully used at Connect 5000 in getting prospects to raise their hands:

- *Introduction*
- *Should we talk?*
- *Should we meet?*
- *Noticed your LinkedIn profile*
- *"Referral's Name" suggested I reach out to you.*
- *Question for you*
- *3 Quick Questions*

Of course, if none of these fits with your particular marketing plan, you are more than welcome to come up with your own. I would recommend that you constantly test and tweak these into something that works for you. Remember the art of email is keeping your communication short, sweet, and to the point. This becomes particularly important as most people read emails on their phones, so brevity is a must. The most effective message is one that a person can read in its entirety on his/her phone screen.

When it comes to crafting your emails, I suggest that you have at least 5 to 7 written and ready so that over a month, you have reached out to someone by phone or email 4-5 times, making up your 8-12 touches per month. If you get no response, recycle them and follow up again in six months.

Another thing to keep in mind when crafting your email is word count. You should be using only 90 to 100 words to craft your message. Get rid of self-promotion and talk about how you can solve a targeted prospect's pain, business problems, and challenges. When we prospect, cold call, and use social media to set sales appointments for technology and consulting companies, we send an email first but follow up with a telephone call. If we get their voicemail, we want to drive them to check their email.

To say that senior executives don't answer their emails or return calls is absolute baloney. They will answer if you have something relevant and timely to say. For example, I emailed the CEO of a $1.16B company in Arkansas. I wasn't expecting a response because he's a very busy executive. But he replied, pointed me in the right direction, and copied the person responsible in a nearly perfect introduction.

Not only do I have numerous other examples of our Connect 5000 team where a phone call started the conversation, but I also have numerous examples where emails opened the door to turn the prospect into a client. Below are some of the actual email templates we use at Connect 5000. As you review them, keep in mind that by now you should know your target audience, your value proposition, and you've done your research on potential prospects.

EMAIL SAMPLE 1:

Subject Line: Introduction

Body:

Prospect First Name,

Hi! I noticed we're 2nd degree LinkedIn connections via {Common LinkedIn connection} and wanted to take the time to reach out to you on behalf of my company, Connect 5000. At Connect 5000, we help software, technology, and consulting companies boost sales revenue with effective lead generation campaigns, sales prospecting strategies, and inside sales management.

More specifically, we shorten sales cycles by generating introductory sales meetings with key decision-makers on your behalf. If hiring an outside firm is cost-prohibitive, we train sales teams on how to prospect and engage effectively to get inside targeted companies.

Simply put, we offer client solutions that lead to results. Those results include:

- Scheduling 110 meetings resulting in $6.1M in new revenue in 13 months for a $30M consulting firm in Atlanta, Georgia.

- Initiating a sales call that resulted in a $27M new contract 7 months later for a $1.B business processing outsourcer.

- Generating over 120 introductory meetings in 6 months for a construction software firm that was acquired by Autodesk.

These numbers serve to prove that we open doors to new opportunities for growth and profitability.

"In today's highly competitive environment, Ray Ruecker is an invaluable resource. Ray removes obstacles; he engages, connects, and communicates a value proposition with laser-like precision. His combination of charm and grit are expressed through his eloquence. Key decision-makers stand up and take notice when Ray calls. I would definitely recommend Ray to any organization that is grappling with how to optimize its resources to break into key accounts. He not only opens the door...he gets you a place at the table." – Keith Sciulli, Scintel Technologies

Even if this isn't a priority today, I promise you'll gain insight from our time together that will put you in a more favorable position when it does become a priority.

How does your calendar look over the next few weeks?

Ray

Email Signature Line

EMAIL SAMPLE 2:

Subject Line: Should we talk?

Body:

Prospect's First Name

Life is busy so I'll make this brief.

Are you aware that about 50% of sales reps don't prospect according to Rain Today? And did you also know that Insidesales.com found it takes between 6 to 8 attempts to reach a decision-maker and that most sales reps only make 1.7 call attempts before giving up?

At Connect 5000, we overcome these hurdles by generating introductory sales meetings with key decision-makers for technology and consulting companies while building a proven record of boosting sales.

- We scheduled over 110 meetings resulting in $6.1M in new revenue in 13 months for a $30M consulting firm in Atlanta.

- We initiated a sales call that resulted in a $27M new contract 7 months later for a $1.B business processing outsourcer.

- We generated over 120 meetings for project executives of the top 300 nationwide construction firms over 6 months. Why did we stop? Autodesk acquired them and the agreement ended.

In short, we've worked with many companies like yours to increase pipelines, shorten sales cycles, and multiply revenue. Let us help your sales team do the same.

"When I was the Chief Marketing Officer at Xangati and Talari, I used Connect 5000 and Ray Ruecker's team to do lead generation and was pleased. After Virtual Instruments acquired us, I moved to Talari in the same role. I reached out to Connect 5000 and have been partnering with his team again

since November 2017 for business development and lead generation efforts and highly recommend his services." – Atchison Frazer, Chief Marketing Officer, and 3X client.

In short, you'll receive value and ideas from our meeting, even if there isn't a next step for me.

With that in mind, are you available to chat in the next few weeks?

Ray

Email Signature Line

 PS: If hiring an outside firm is cost-prohibitive, we also train sales teams on how to prospect and engage effectively to get inside targeted companies.

EMAIL SAMPLE 3:

Subject Line: 3 Quick Questions

Body:

Prospect's First Name,

Is your marketing department flooding your sales team with inbound leads?

Is your sales team overwhelmed with referrals and introductions from their networking efforts?

If not, have you considered hiring an outside outbound lead generation firm this year?

Ray

Email Signature Line

EMAIL SAMPLE 4:

Subject Line: Noticed Your LinkedIn Profile

Body:

Prospect's First Name,

I recently viewed your LinkedIn profile with interest and thought it might make sense to chat. All I need is 5 minutes to pose two quick questions to you regarding your outbound sales team.

How does your schedule look in the next week or two?

Thanks,

Ray

Email Signature Line

EMAIL SAMPLE 5:

Subject line: Feedback

Body:

Prospect's First Name,

I've reached out a few times to discuss Connect 5000's lead generation and training services and how companies like Company X, Company Y, and Company Z partner with us to shorten sales cycles and multiply revenue more effectively than ever before.

As I understand it's not always convenient to reply to a sales call, I wanted to make a response as painless as possible. Please reply to this email with a single-digit if applicable:

1. I'm interested, let's find 15 minutes to connect in the next few days.

2. I'm interested but this isn't a top priority, check back in 2-3 months.

3. Not sure what you're talking about. Please send information.

4. I'm not the right person. You should contact _____

5. I'm not interested, please take me off your list.

Thanks for making the effort to respond!

Ray

This email is my final outreach attempt before remarketing after an appropriate amount of time has passed. And believe it or not, a good number of executives respond they aren't interested, point me in another direction, or start the discovery process with me.

SCOREBOARD SUMMARY:

When creating an email campaign, keep your message clear and concise. Establish your reason for reaching out quickly and use a mutual connection if you have one. This strategy is key to keeping the attention of overwhelmed prospects.

CHAPTER 8

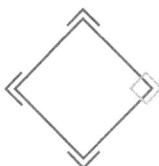

CHAPTER 9:
Making LinkedIn Work for You

"Only God can do a miracle, but most of them also seem connected to very hard work on the part of human beings." – former Senator Bill Frist

Since 2002, LinkedIn has been a key part of my strategy to foster new connections and revive the old. If you don't currently have an account, it's time to create one. For those of you who are unfamiliar with this service, think of it as the professional version of Facebook. But in this case, it is used as a way to leverage your business network to bring in more clients. As mentioned previously, there is a strategy for maximizing communication. LinkedIn is no exception.

In truth, there are countless books and resources on how to best leverage and navigate LinkedIn so I'll keep this chapter short. Begin by signing up for the free LinkedIn version even though there is also a paid version. Make sure that you upload a current profile picture that is no more than ten years old. And when you fill out your profile experience, highlight accomplishments that will make you stand out from other profiles. You don't want to exaggerate but it is always appropriate to highlight your accomplishments as long as you are truthful and reasonable.

When using LinkedIn, it is also important to list out the pain, problems, and challenges that you solve. Include metrics and success for past and present clients. If you increased their revenue, decreased their expenses, improved efficiency, you need to mention it. And when you do, do your best to use percentages and dollar savings in your description, because we all will respond to someone's concerted effort to not only identify but solve our problems. So much so, we will spend more to make sure the outcome (and/or problem solved) is accomplished. Every day, this might look a little differently than in the business world. But it exists, nonetheless. We need to look no further than my own medical care - or lack thereof.

I'll admit to being a typical guy. I don't go see the doctor unless something's wrong. Until recently, I hadn't seen a doctor since June 2005, when my wife strongly suggested I go in for a yearly physical. We had just gotten married so for her peace of mind, I set an appointment and received a clean bill of health from my doctor.

But then I began struggling with sinus infections and allergies. And truthfully? I felt miserable. So, I found an allergist who made some excellent recommendations to help alleviate my symptoms. It took me being miserable and in pain to finally call the doctor and seek a solution. But what does this have to do with sales hunting and sales prospecting?

Most prospects tend to buy solutions that solve their business "pain" before they buy solutions that will enhance their company. In other words, we will reach for an aspirin to treat our headaches before we will buy vitamins to make ourselves feel even better.

When reaching out to prospects, formulate your questions in a way that uncovers their pain and then treat their pain with your product or service. It is also important to make sure you aren't too slick when it comes to using metrics. For example, if you helped increase a company's revenue by 10%, use something like 9.9% or 9.8.% It's more believable and helps to build your credibility.

Another must is to include testimonials in your profile. Get testimonials from clients. Get testimonials from colleagues. And if they are too busy, offer to draft one for them if need be. In my experience, when I have offered to draft one for clients, they often just cut and paste it and add additional relevant information. So, help them get the ball rolling. Like metrics, testimonials give you credibility and people are more inclined to believe what you are selling.

Remember, no matter how much technology exists, connecting and selling is interacting with people. People may look you up on LinkedIn before responding to you. Why? They simply want to get a sense of who you are personally and professionally.

Not only is LinkedIn an effective marketing platform, but it is also a wonderful research tool. Keep in mind, however, that I am not advocating that you spend an enormous amount of time on research as an excuse to avoid prospecting. But it doesn't hurt to take a few minutes and look at your target's profile. You may find some helpful information that you can use to disarm your prospect.

For example, you may find out that you both attended the same university. Or that you are both avid fans of the same NFL or NBA team. Or that he/she is on the board of a non-profit you support. The key is to find common ground quickly and use it to your advantage. LinkedIn is not only free advertising but it is also a great connecting and prospecting tool that you can filter based on several criteria.

For example, let's say I want to reach out to Vice Presidents of Sales for software, technology, and consulting companies in Kansas City-based on first and second connections. LinkedIn will create a list for me. While you can upgrade to the Sales Navigator or Premium option, LinkedIn alone can be an effective and inexpensive way to help find potential clients quickly. Another advantage of LinkedIn is that you can reference your first and second-degree connections in your introduction, be it by email or voicemail.

In other words, if I am reaching out to a company and we have a mutual connection, I will not only identify myself but also our mutual connection, both by phone and email. I might begin with something like:

"Hey, Bob, Ray Ruecker with Connect 5000, I am connected to you on LinkedIn through <insert name here> who just so happens to be a current client of mine."

Even though there is always the chance that the person doesn't know the connection directly, the probability that he/she might is always worth the risk. John Nemo, a national expert, and author on how to leverage LinkedIn, wrote *LinkedIn Riches* which is arguably the best-written resource on how to best use LinkedIn to grow your business. If you are unfamiliar with his work, now is the time to read his book. Because you *can g*enerate a lot of business on LinkedIn with its search function and ability to leverage who you know. If time is limited, use this tool often and with purpose.

Another reason to use LinkedIn and pay attention to your newsfeed is that it might reveal information that will help you in your prospecting efforts. In the past, I reached out to the CEO of a technology company here in the Kansas City metro. I sent him a personalized gift that he passed on to the VP of Marketing. The VP of Marketing then reached out to me and we exchanged several emails. Following our exchange, she sent me to one of her direct reports. The direct report and I had a few conversations by phone but the result was a no. No problem. It happens all the time so I closed the file. But a few months later, I noticed on LinkedIn that this direct report was no longer with the company. She had moved on to another company. I found the previous email exchange with the Marketing VP, reached out, and set up a time to meet in person. We discussed their needs and they were open to using us. Long story short, we agreed and we both signed off on a proposal. As such, it's always important to remember the path to home plate takes a detour now and then.

The final thing we will explore regarding LinkedIn is whether or not it is in your best interest professionally to grow your number of connections into the thousands. The truth is many people on LinkedIn have an extraordinarily high number of connections. But I intentionally keep my connections at a minimum. At present, I only have around 800 because I intentionally limit my connections to only people with whom I have had a quality conversation or interaction.

What is my reason for doing so?

Simply put, I don't want to appear ignorant and foolish if someone in my network asks me to make an introduction and I know nothing about him/her. That kind of connection is meaningless. According to anthropologist Robin Dunbar, humans can only comfortably maintain 150 stable relationships. And I concur. In today's frenzied business world, it's hard to stay in contact with everyone.

If you still doubt the power of LinkedIn, consider this. In the past two months, two separate LinkedIn connections with whom I had worked in the past reached out to me. One connection's company got acquired and he introduced me to his new CEO. The other was working at a different company and was striking out on his own. Although I was humbled they both thought enough of me to reconnect, it is this very scenario that best conveys the true power of LinkedIn. And while I am not an expert by any means, there are also countless resources out on the Internet on how to leverage LinkedIn to increase your sales or land a new career.

At Connect 5000, we leverage Linkedin when connecting or prospecting in the following ways:

LinkedIn Inmails - If you upgrade to a monthly paid premium account, you can send emails to your targeted prospect even if you aren't connected. If the prospect rejects your Inmail, it gets credited back to you. The only challenge is that Inmails are quickly becoming inundated with marketers and become akin to an overflowing email inbox. Although the cost of LinkedIn premium was $59.99 per month at the time of this writing, it more than pays for itself if you get even one new client.

Voicemail - If I'm trying to connect with an executive who I've never spoken with before, I use one of the following two approaches when leaving a voicemail.

"Hi (Prospect's First Name), Ray Ruecker with Connect 5000. I'm following up on an email I sent you recently. I'm connected to you on LinkedIn via (Mutual Connection's Name) and thought it might make sense for us to talk."

OR

"Hi (Prospect's First Name), Ray Ruecker with Connect 5000. I'm following up on an email I sent you recently. I'm connected to you on LinkedIn via (Mutual Connection's Name), a past / present client of mine."

In addition to using one of the above voicemails, add relevant information, or share a success story and leave your phone number twice.

Live Connection - If I caught my targeted prospect on the phone, I use the following script:

"Hi (Prospect's First Name), Ray Ruecker with Connect 5000. I'm following up on an email I sent you recently. I noticed your LinkedIn profile because we're both connected to (Mutual Connection's Name), a current client of mine, and thought it made sense for us to talk. Did I catch you in a meeting?"

Snail Mail/Email - If I send out direct mail via the U.S. Postal Service or an email, here's the very first sentence I use following the salutation:

"Hi! I noticed we're 2nd degree LinkedIn connections via (Prospect's full name), a client of mine."

Another helpful hint if you're a solopreneur, business owner, or company that performs functions on an outsourced basis is to go to the "Jobs" section in LinkedIn, type in key search terms and apply to these "positions" even though you're a "company." Why? Because there's already a defined need with a public company. Some will absolutely not outsource to meet that need but others will. Offer to perform the function temporarily until they find a permanent solution. In the end, they may hire you for the long-term. Remember, the goal is to score the run, not fixate on the way it must be done.

SCOREBOARD SUMMARY:

A meaningful LinkedIn connection will always work in your favor. Keep things streamlined, pay attention to the things that matter, and be vigilant in watching your feed for important information. It may give you a chance to get back in the door with a company whose decision-makers had initially said, "No."

CHAPTER 9

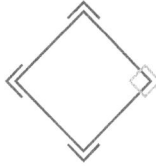

CHAPTER 10:
Rediscovering the Art of Snail Mail

"Self-discipline is the ability to make yourself do something you don't necessarily want to do, to get a result you would really like to have."
– Andy Andrews

When I became a dad, I realized that one of the greatest challenges in early parenthood is finding reliable and quality childcare. We have been fortunate, however, in that not only is our regular "date night" babysitter amazing with our kids, but our relationship with her has also spanned over a decade. Naturally, when a colleague of mine reached out to me looking for a childcare referral, I didn't hesitate to give him her name.

A few days later, we received a small thank you card in the mail along with a restaurant gift card as our babysitter's way of thanking us for referring her to my colleague. Not only was it a completely unexpected gesture but it also confirmed that our trust in her had been well-placed.

While everyone in sales knows a new client or referral warrants a written thank you note, very few of us write one. We often get so busy we simply forget it makes a difference. And yet, this meaningful gesture on the part of our babysitter serves to remind me of the subsequent advantages to sending a "thank you" in the mail:

1. Because it is such a rare form of communication, snail mail will always stand out and set you apart from other companies.

2. Snail mail is often unexpected so its arrival is likely to brighten the recipient's day.

3. A gesture of goodwill serves as money in the bank. (How likely is it that am I going to refer our sitter to other friends who need occasional babysitting help? The answer is very likely.)

The reality is that direct mail is a dying art. This is in large part because social media marketing and email are simply easier to use. But it is also the very reason that personalized, thoughtful snail mail can be effective and stand out among your competitors. Even though the phone, email, and LinkedIn are most people's preferred form of communication, other prospects will raise their hands and say, "I'm interested in talking," based solely on something they received in the mail.

Case in point: In August 2016, I received an email from a Senior Vice President of Sales here in Kansas City. I had reached out via the phone and email. He hadn't received or responded to either of my attempts. He emailed me because he had received my letter and business card which began the conversation. The email read:

Hi Ray,

I am in the market for doing some outbound calling/appointment setting. Let me know if you have some time to talk – XXXX is in Overland Park.

Jim XXXX

SVP Sales

(Company Name)

As with everything, there are a few general guidelines you should follow as you are creating your direct mail campaign. To begin, whenever you use mail to prospect, make sure you use an envelope with a real stamp. Next, handwrite the prospect's name, address, company, city, state, and zip code. This alone will pique interest as a handwritten note alone will spark a prospect's curiosity. It is also the only form of communication in which you don't need to be short, sweet, and to the point. While a letter to a prospect shouldn't be particularly long-winded, it is still acceptable to make it at least a few pages in length. Last but not least, sign your name at the bottom and enclose your business card. As you create your mailers, be sure to have a few templates that resemble your sales campaign emails and phone scripts. There is no need to draft a brand new letter for every new prospect. Simply create a few variations for different points of entry based on sales situations. And if you cringe at the thought of writing notes yourself, Send Out Cards or Mail Lift are companies that provide personalized handwritten cards or letters for a fee.

Think of it this way: What is easier to delete? A voicemail, an email, or a letter? It's really easy to delete a voicemail. It's also really easy to delete an email. But someone has to make an intentional effort to throw your letter away. You never know when a targeted executive needs a distraction and decides to go through his mail only to find your envelope.

Does it work every time? No.

But is it worth your time? Absolutely.

When you follow up direct mail by phone, your voicemail might be a little bit different than if you had sent an email. You should reference the letter and gently remind the prospect to look for it just in case he/she didn't receive it. It may be stuck on his/her desk or in the mailroom. But regardless of where it is, never assume that the prospect has received it when drafting your sales talk track.

Just as with any sales tool, don't ever be afraid to use humor as a way to connect with prospective clients. It gives you another way to score when nothing else is getting you past first base. John Ruhlin, a corporate gifting specialist, tells the story of a guy trying to get the attention of a major executive in his industry. He had tried anything and everything with no response. But then he got clever when he sent the executive a ten-dollar mini trash can along with a note that said:

"I wanted to make it easier for you to ignore my letter this time around."

Sometime later, this gentleman received a phone call from a private number. And wouldn't you know it: "Hi there. Is this Mr. (name withheld)? You had me in stitches! I admire your perseverance and creativity. Let's talk!"

Another client of mine who has a managed services provider company in Atlanta sends a sample-sized aspirin taped to their introductory letter. The headline reads "Is your IT department causing you headaches?" While this may sound corny, when was the last time you received medicine in the mail? The bottom line is it pays to be memorable.

SCOREBOARD SUMMARY:

When you are casting a wide net, you must accept that each method and style of communication has a unique target base. The same proves true for snail mail. Don't be afraid to get personal. Trying an old strategy could very well bring about new opportunities.

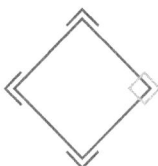

CHAPTER 11:
Unexpected Ways to Forge Connections

"It's better to do something about one thing than nothing about everything."
– Mike Ashcraft

For years, a well-known story has circulated the business world about a person who sent a shoebox with one shoe to a company's executive decision-maker with a note saying, "We'd like to get our foot in the door."

It's smart. It's clever. It's creative, albeit now overused. Nevertheless, it is a great example as to why it is important to continually generate creative ideas as to how to get in the door if the phone, email, snail-mail, and LinkedIn isn't working for you. I have only one guideline for unconventional sales openers: Be creative but *don't* be boring or obnoxious.

One of the easiest ways you can do this is by sending the company's decision-maker(s) a handwritten note. Let me qualify this by saying I am not suggesting you write a business letter. Instead, send a postcard or write a personal note and enclose your business card. Keep it short, sweet, and to the point. It could even be something as simple as, **"Hey (Prospect's First Name), Ray Ruecker with Connect 5000. I'd like to chat with you about <>. Please give me a call."**

Another hook that is simple and fairly inexpensive is to include a $5 Starbucks gift card with a note that reads, **"Here's a cup of coffee on me. Could you call me when you have 5 minutes please?"**

A more expensive hook that I use frequently involves Cutco, an online, customized knife company. I have the prospect's name engraved on the handle and then I have it gift-wrapped and sent with a little note that says, **"Can we "carve" out a few minutes to chat?"** A word of caution, however, is to avoid engraving your company's name or your name on the handle. Because without a doubt, they'll remember who the knife came from for the rest of their lives.

Another option is to purchase stopwatches off of Amazon (typically in the $5-10 range.) Then, attach a note to it that asks, **"Hey Mr. Prospect, can I have five minutes to chat?"** For an even more select few, I have sent alcohol. But make sure you know enough about the prospect to ensure they drink. On the off chance they don't, you risk offending them.

Another creative prospecting tool includes finding what nonprofits your prospect supports. Typically, these will be listed in his/her Linked-In profile where they may be listed as a volunteer or serve on the board. Then, donate on his/her behalf and send a note that says, **"Hey, I like what you are doing. I donated $X in your honor. Could we carve out some time to talk?"** Not terribly long ago, I noticed a local prospect was on the executive board for the local Make-A-Wish Foundation. I made a $100 donation in his name and forwarded him the receipt. Subsequently, the Chief Sales Officer agreed to meet. I'm not suggesting you spend $100 every time but if it is a potentially high average sale, consider it the cost of doing business. Even if they don't respond, guess what? You've donated to a good cause.

Expert Michael Katz recommends using www.discountmugs.com where you have the option to engrave your company logo on one side. Katz's further recommends putting this on the other side of the mug: "If _____ is causing you to drink, contact us at _____." It is important to clarify that the first blank is to be used to name the business problem they may be experiencing. Not only is it memorable, but it will likely also be something that your prospect will use regularly.

Two companies that also provide a unique product that works well to pique a prospect's interest are Potato Parcel and www.sendaball.com. Potato Parcel sends an actual potato in the mail with a short message. And SendaBall delivers a message to the recipient on a colorful bouncy ball. Both are unexpected, unique, and provide the perfect opportunity to create a hook that stands out and allows you to round the bases.

SCOREBOARD SUMMARY:

Whatever you use to pique a potential client's interest, make sure it's unexpected and grabs his/her attention without being too crazy or unconventional. Will it always work? Sometimes it will. Sometimes it won't. But the reality is, you won't know until you try.

CHAPTER 11

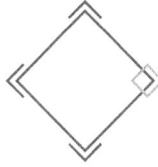

CHAPTER 12:
Finding a Needle in a Haystack

"Our greatest weakness lies in giving up. The most certain way to succeed is always to try just one more time." – Thomas Edison

For seven years, my wife worked as a paralegal at the same law firm. But in July 2013, she left the firm to stay home with our then 4-year-old daughter and 1-year-old son. Not terribly long after she left, I decided to call her direct number just for grins and discovered that my wife's voicemail message was still being used and made no mention that she had left.

This brief exercise taught me to always take the next step in confirming a prospect's information. When I use the contact information found on a company's website to reach a prospect, I always make it a point to email the potential client as well. Sometimes, an email auto-responder is the only way to confirm whether or not he/she is still with the company.

Following a recent CRM cleanup, I discovered that 19-22% of my prospects were no longer there. I'm talking about C-level Officers, Vice Presidents, and Directors. Not exactly mid-level people. So when in doubt, call the main number, ask to speak to your targeted prospect and if the receptionist says that person is no longer there, it's one less person with whom you have to follow up.

While there are a great many challenges to prospecting, perhaps the most prevalent and time-consuming is finding accurate contact information. Up until May 2019, I religiously used a service called Data.com (previously known as Jigsaw.) It was acquired by Salesforce.com in 2010 and active for several years. In many ways, it was a Wikipedia of executives' contact information. The concept was simple. The service allowed users to input a prospect's information, giving them five points. For example, if a prospect switched jobs or received a promotion, you could update the prospect and gain five points. On the other hand, if you needed information for another prospect, you would "spend" five points to access the data. And while they offered both a paid and unpaid version of the service, I always had enough points credited to me so I never even had to consider purchasing points. Unfortunately, Data.com was eliminated in May 2019.

But if you simply google "Data.com competitors," you will find a large number of user-friendly alternatives, including but not limited to Lead411, ZoomInfo, and DiscoverOrg. Another alternative that I personally use and endorse is Hunter.io. This tool will spit out email addresses affiliated with a prospect's domain and verified source links as long as you can provide the domain name. However, it doesn't provide you with as many phone numbers as it does other information. If you are having a hard time finding an email address or contact information, this service is invaluable. Moreover, you are allowed a limited number of searches for free before having to pay for their service.

Even if you are employed by an organization whose marketing department doesn't provide these types of tools, that's okay. A baseball player doesn't exclusively rely on the team's training program--he has to invest his own time, energy, and often, financial resources to make sure he is competing at top performance. Even though he's not a baseball player, superstar basketball player Lebron James reportedly spends $1.5M to take care of his body.[22] In the same way, invest in yourself and demonstrate initiative by using a service that will not only make you more efficient but also more profitable. Sam Richter in his book "Take the Cold Out of Cold Calling" provides several additional ways to access information online, as well as how to research prospects before reaching out to them. If you haven't read it, it is more than worth your time. And if you are smart enough to put into practice what Richter recommends, you will inevitably increase your number of connections and in turn, your sales revenue. As you go through the process of digging for contact information, I would recommend the following system:

1. Go to the targeted company's website. Then click on the "About Us" or "Leadership" or "Staff" tab and begin using your detective chops as well as some old-fashioned common sense. While in some cases you may find the company's main number, keep in mind that there is a new trend among tech companies to eliminate their main number from the website altogether.

2. If you are unable to find the information you need on the website, then go to LinkedIn and filter your search by company name/ potential title(s) and see what information pops up.

3. Next, use a similar service like Hunter.io to retrieve executives' contact information.

4. And in the end, if all else fails and you have to rely solely on email, try different email format combinations and you may get lucky.

If you don't want the tedium of the tips and tricks above, there are a couple of formats that are most typical of business email addresses. Most often, it is the first initial, last name @ domain.com.

Just like my email address: rruecker@connect5000.com.

Other times, the format might be the first name.last name @ domain. com OR first name underscore, last name@domain.com. If you still get bounce backs or undeliverable emails, consider the following formulas:

- firstnamelastname

- firstname

- lastname

- firstinitiallastname

- firstnameinitial

- firstinitial.lastname

- firstname.initial

If you have to guess which format a particular executive email address uses, put their potential email address in the To: line and then blind copy a few other combinations. That way you don't have to wonder which one of the formats is legitimate. All you have to do is wait to see which one bounces back.

SCOREBOARD SUMMARY:
No matter what tool you use to find elusive information, always pair it with a tracker. It will make the most of your time, energy, and effort. And if you cannot find a prospect's phone number, always send an email. In some cases, it may be a long shot but it's better than not attempting contact at all.

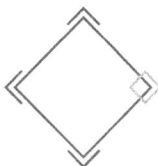

CHAPTER 13:
Making the Most Out of a Live Connection

"The question isn't who is going to let me; it's who is going to stop me."
– Ayn Rand

In baseball, a player gets three strikes to make a connection with the ball, assuming it's in the strike zone. But when targeting senior executives, you typically only have one chance to get your proverbial foot in the door.

Between their overscheduled workdays and limited attention spans, executives are often overwhelmed by the sheer amount of work their job requires. But on those occasions that you do catch a prospect live, it is just as important to have a prepared and purposeful script or talk track as it is with voicemail. Moreover, it is of continued importance that you also show respect and professionalism by always asking for the prospect's permission to chat.

With that being said, it is still important to remain alert and do your best to avoid just going through the motions. Sometimes, we leave so many voicemails that when a prospect answers, we are caught off guard and come across as unprepared and inarticulate. While some so-called "experts" recommend launching into your pitch the minute you hear a "Hello," I disagree. The prospect, even though he/she answered, may still be in the middle of something that demands his/her time. Or maybe they answered only because they were expecting an important call and mistakenly thought you were it. But no matter what the case may be, it is important to ascertain that from the get-go.

For anyone who still doubts my logic, consider this: we wouldn't interrupt our colleagues at work without showing some professional courtesy. Nor would we barge into other people's offices without an invitation. It only makes sense that we should extend the same courtesy to people with whom we eventually want to do business.

Another word of caution if your prospect answers are to avoid asking, **"How are you?"** In most situations, this question is a turn-off as it is often overused and trite. Instead try asking, **"Did I catch you at a good time?"** Or **"Are you in a meeting?"** It's a yes or no question that demands very little time and effort to answer. And if you show professional courtesy and respect, the targeted executive will more than likely signal you one way or another to proceed or call back at a later time. Then depending on the answer, you can move forward by introducing yourself, sharing your value proposition, and asking open-ended questions and/or reference previous communication.

But keep in mind that open-ended questions need planning, consideration, and should follow these general guidelines:

1. Keep questions open-ended whose sole purpose is to keep your conversation on track.
2. Avoid interrogating your prospect. Instead, begin your conversations with personal thought-provoking questions.
3. Practice asking these questions with a colleague as a way to ensure they blend easily into client conversations.
4. Create questions that don't over qualify your prospect. (The goal is to get a meeting, not sell him/her on the spot.)
5. Questions should strive to uncover the prospect's pain, problems, and challenges.

6. Save questions that are meant to uncover budget, authority, need, and timeline (BANT) for after you gain their trust.

Samples of scripts that follow the aforementioned guidelines are:

Sample Live Approaches:

If a targeted prospect answers your phone call, there are several ways to open the conversation, depending on your type of connection and situation. Here are some examples:

If you're reaching out to an executive with no connection or common ground:

"Hi (Prospect First Name), Ray Ruecker with Connect 5000. I'm following up on an email I sent you recently. I noticed your LinkedIn profile and thought it made sense to chat. Did I catch you in a meeting?"

(Wait for them to respond.)

"We've helped companies like yours accomplish ABC, resulting in XYZ. I thought we might be able to accomplish similar results for you. But to begin, I would like to ask you a few questions."

(At this point, ask open-ended question numbers 1 and 2. Then, depending on how they respond, ask some of the following questions to get them to go further.)

"How so? How long has this gone on? Tell me more. Could you please elaborate on that?"

If you have a referral within an organization:

"Hi (Prospect First Name), Ray Ruecker with Connect 5000. I'm following up on an email I sent you recently. (Referral Full Name) in your firm suggested I reach out to you. Did I catch you in a meeting?"

(Then pause and wait for your target to answer. If you get the go-ahead, then proceed.)

"We've helped companies like yours accomplish XYZ by X% or Y$. I'd like to ask a few questions to see if it makes sense to chat further."

If and only if there's interest, ask how the person's calendar is to meet, visit, or chat in the next few weeks. Give them plenty of options so you have a better chance of fitting into their already busy schedule.

If an Executive Assistant in C-Suite referred you:

"Hi (Prospect First Name), Ray Ruecker with Connect 5000. I'm following up on an email I sent you recently. (Executive Assistant's Full Name) in (C-level Executive's Full Name) office suggested I reach out to you. Did I catch you in a meeting?

Open-ended questions:

If you're stuck with some open-ended questions to come up with on your own, try these to get started:

- "Is (business problem) a current challenge in 2020 and beyond?"
- "Is _____ a pain or problem?"
- "Is _____ a priority?"
- "How so? Tell me more. How long has this been going on?"

Mutual LinkedIn Connection:

"Hi (Prospect First Name), Ray Ruecker with Connect 5000. I'm following up on an email I sent you recently. I noticed your LinkedIn profile because we're both connected to (LinkedIn Connection's Full Name). Did I catch you in a meeting?"

Don't automatically assume the prospect knows the name you just mentioned. As an alternative, you may ask after you name drop: "Does his/

her name ring a bell or sound familiar?"

Past or Present Client Connection:

"Hi (Prospect First Name,) Ray Ruecker with Connect 5000. I'm following up on an email I sent you recently. I noticed your LinkedIn profile because we're both connected to (LinkedIn Connection's Full Name,) a past/present client of mine. Did I catch you in a meeting?"

(Wait for a response.)

"We helped (LinkedIn Name's) company accomplish XYZ. I'd like to ask a few questions to see if it makes sense to chat further."

(Ask open-ended questions 1, 2, and 3.)

If a prospect returns your call:

Sometimes our diligence pays off and the targeted prospect decides to return our call. And if that happens, exchange pleasantries and get to the point. But if you get stuck, lose your train of thought, or simply forgot who this person is or what the call was about, ask this simple question:

"(Prospect's First Name), thank you for returning my call. If you don't mind me asking, what prompted you to call me back / return my call?"

(Wait for a response or if he/she seems unsure about his answer, ask the question a different way.)

"(Prospect's First Name,) you're busy and you get calls all the time, what was it about my voicemail that caught your attention and returned my call?"

Remember that something in your message triggered them to call you back. Make sure you find out what it was before you get too far into the conversation.

But as I mentioned earlier, make sure you don't over qualify the prospect. Keep in mind that your first objective is simply to get in the door. It is not intended to be an interrogation. And if a prospect agrees to meet with you, take what he/she gives you. If he wants to chat by phone, great. If she wants to meet face-to-face, even better. Your goal is simply to get your foot in the door.

Zoom calls and similar video services skyrocketed during the COVID-19 pandemic because they allowed for more direct communication and provided similar benefits as a face-to-face conversation. I recommend virtual meetings to allow you to see your client's facial expression and personality in real-time rather than just hearing their voice. Take whatever the prospect will give you.

Case in point? My wife and I make it a consistent habit to give away 10% of our income to our church, charities, and other organizations that cross our path. Recently, we received a letter from her college alma mater asking for money. It was in no way unexpected as we receive one every year. But it has always served as a reminder that we will be getting a phone call from them in the near future.

This has allowed us to agree on a dollar amount so that when they call, the conversation is short and sweet. It is also why on one occasion I took their call at a time that was typically not the best for us. I assumed it would be quick and painless and that we could quickly move onto the rest of our nightly routine.

The caller sounded scripted, canned, and mechanical. I finally cut her off and told her the specific size of our donation and that we'd send it in that week. But instead of taking the time to listen, she ignored the cue and kept talking. Unfortunately, the caller was more concerned about getting done with her script than she was efficiently ending the call with a donation that she could add to her credit.

How guilty are we at missing cues and overtalking the sale?

I know I am.

When a prospect says "yes" to you about meeting for the first time or moving forward, recognize the cues, and then gladly and graciously accept the next step. It's okay to exchange pleasantries, but don't talk yourself out of an initial meeting or new client. And keep in mind that just because we want to share something with the client doesn't mean he/she wants to hear it. By sharing too much information, we may inadvertently cause the prospect to change his/her mind.

For example, I have a client who I didn't meet face-to-face for over a year and a half even though we lived in the same town. Because he traveled and rarely had any downtime, we always talked by phone. When we finally met, I even made a joke of it and said, "Hey, it only took a year and a half to meet you in person." Per my point, take what the prospect gives you. And if you can set up a coffee, lunch, or drinks, be willing to drive their direction and meet them on their terms.

Another effective communication strategy when talking to a prospect live is to tell them client success stories with metrics. You might use a talk track similar to "**Hey Johnny, I helped a software company like yours increase their revenue by 12%. I don't know if I can help you but would like to share what I did to see if it might be of interest to you. How does your calendar look over the next few weeks?**" Remember to be as specific as possible when using numbers as they make you sound more credible.

Also, never avoid using your personal story to connect with your prospects. It may be best to shy away from doing so on the first call. But as you engage with prospective clients, if you hear them ask you, "What's your background?" Respond to them by walking through that open door and make a meaningful connection. As they become comfortable with your company, service, or price, clients will want to get to know you, the salesperson, as a person, minus the projected image you've given them. So always have an answer ready. It doesn't need to be emotional vomit or a 10-minute speech, but give them a glimpse into your personal life. For example, I often tell prospects I have a background in construction software. Or I tell them I'm Asian with a white guy's voice because I was adopted from Vietnam at the age of one. It's short, to the point, and ultimately, memorable.

SCOREBOARD SUMMARY:
In the age of technology and social media, people still buy from other people. Don't be afraid to weave your personal story into your conversations and reveal a little of your personality to your clients. In choosing your words and content wisely during a live connection, you give yourself a greater chance at a follow-up conversation.

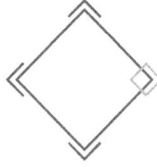

CHAPTER 14:
Utilizing the Face-to-Face Advantage

"Learn to listen. Opportunity sometimes knocks very softly."
– H. Jackson Brown Jr.

Because technology provides us with the ability to virtually "meet" and communicate, it is entirely possible to have a solid business relationship without meeting a client in person. But in our attempts to build and nurture connection, nothing builds it quicker than face-to-face contact even if it requires some travel and expense.

Several months ago, I flew to Chicago to attend a sales lunch along with my business development representative. He had successfully reached out to a prospect who had agreed to meet us for lunch and bring his marketing executive with him. Because this company is a $1B+ accounting and consulting firm with offices nationwide, we both saw the value of meeting this firm face-to-face. I flew to Chicago, spent the night in a hotel, and attended lunch the following day. Between airfare, lodging, and meals, the cost of the trip was about $700.

Was I guaranteed a client? Absolutely not. But we saw the value of meeting face-to-face, knowing there is no substitute like sharing a meal with a potential prospect. We talked about scope and numbers, and then parted ways.

Yes, conference calls are more efficient, but if a firm gets multiple calls, you're just another voice, name, and company to them. Meeting in person makes you memorable and makes the connection stronger (assuming you add value.)

A few weeks later, we agreed to terms and were looking at a start date in June. Unfortunately, the office we were helping had no one in place to run the meetings we would be scheduling for them. But by August, they had hired someone exclusively for that role and we secured them as a client.

Takeaway #1: Always keep your sales pipeline full and keep prospecting. Even if you agree on terms, sign a contract, and are seemingly ready to go, the client may have some internal delays on their end over which you have no control.

Takeaway #2: Companies with multiple offices talk to each other. You're thinking "Duh, of course!" Yet, we forget these simple facts. You never know when one lunch can lead to an expanded scope with a company.

In this case, another branch from the same company called us only two weeks after we signed the contract with the Chicago office. It seems this branch was facing the same challenges and had somehow connected with our contact. We had an initial call about our services, then another conference call with three of their team members. Shortly after, they secured our services as well.

While effective in creating connection, face-to-face contact may come with a considerable investment. When trying to decide whether out-of-town travel is worth the expense, it is always prudent to weigh your options. Not long ago, I met with a VP of Sales of a large health benefits organization. She and I discussed whether the first sales meeting should be face-to-face or by phone since her target state of Iowa was only three hours away. Having had success with both options, she wanted my opinion. I considered the words of Mark Hunter from his book ***"High-Profit Prospecting: Powerful Strategies to Find the Best Leads and Drive***

Breakthrough Sales Results" when deciding whether or not I would encourage her to make the trip:

"Although it's never easy to know exactly when to visit a potential cold-calling customer, a rule of thumb I tell people is that it's perfectly acceptable to use the telephone to take the customer to the close if it will require you to fly to meet the customer in person. If the customer is in your city, then you need to visit the customer as soon as you've identified them as a probable customer or a suspect that has significant profit potential. When you do fly to meet the customer, it's best to do it just before finalizing the sale.

Meeting in person with the customer will allow you to further exemplify why you're the one with whom he/she should work. It will allow you to deepen the relationship and in turn, deepen the need the customer has for working with you. Never jump in your car or jump on an airplane to go chase a hunch. Your time is far more valuable than that. If you're not professional enough to be able to fill your pipeline with quality leads and prospects in addition to being capable of creating need and pain with a prospect, then you shouldn't be selling." [23]

While I agree with most of what Hunter says, I also gave my client this direction: If a potential prospect is within 1 hour of driving, I'd ask for a meeting face-to-face. If the meeting is successful, you've invested 3 hours of your time: 1-hour driving there, 1 hour of meeting, and 1 hour of driving back. When I have prospects that close, I make it a point to meet with them face-to-face because it is nearly always worthwhile to see their body language first hand.

But we live in the real world, not a bubble. Things come up—funerals, fires, family emergencies, client issues, etc.—and you will find there are legitimate reasons as to why a prospect has to cancel or reschedule. But if you have driven a certain amount of distance before they cancel, keep in mind you've wasted time that you'll never get back. To me, it's not the issue of the cost of gas, it is the cost of my time. I can always go out and make more money but I can never regain my time.

At Connect 5000, we conduct business with technology and consulting companies nationwide. While we have clients we've never met in person, my goal eventually is to hop on a plane and see them at least once a year face-to-face. But with the technology and tools we have available, there are several cost-effective ways to chat with potential clients in a personal way.

It is perfectly acceptable to have your first meeting through teleconference. It's efficient and if you're doing your job properly, you can qualify needs and challenges within the first 15 minutes. Once someone has agreed to a conference call, I'll send a calendar email invite using Zoom or Unite Conferencing as an option for our conferencing medium. But if they don't have an account, the phone is still an effective tool. The only exception is if your dream client reaches out to you and requests a meeting in person. In that case, hop on the first plane available, confidently knowing there are always exceptions to any rule and trusting that sometimes scoring is worth the extra cost.

SCOREBOARD SUMMARY:
When deciding if traveling to visit a prospect makes sense, be diligent, discerning, and always factor in the potential lifetime value of the client. You will then have a quantifiable way to determine if a face-to-face connection is worth the expense.

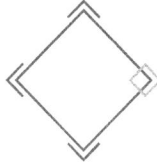

CHAPTER 15:
It May Be Time to Write a New Song

"Excellence is doing ordinary things extraordinarily well." – John W. Gardner

I've always been a big fan of Garth Brooks. In large part, it is nostalgia. His music is one of the few things my late father and I shared. It's also why whenever Garth is in town, I make it a point to do my best to see him perform even when tickets are hard to find.

Over the years, it has become clear as to why people love Garth and flock to his concerts in droves. He is the master of singing singable songs. While a little obvious, this gift is of importance because it is something many artists lack. Simply put, Garth's lyrics are written in such a way that they are easy to recall. In many ways, the last concert I attended was more of a giant sing-along rather than a performance.

Consider this for a moment: How singable are your company's "lyrics?" Can others easily recite what you do and the services you provide? If they cannot, it is time to write a new song, one that is sequential as well as memorable.

Whenever I am asked, "How many attempts and how far apart should I reach out and connect with a prospect?" I always give the direct and forthcoming response, "It depends." Because the truth is every sales resource answers the question differently and some authors even answer multiple ways depending on the circumstances. The reality is the more you tailor your answer to any given situation, the more successful you will be. Remember, it takes at least 8 to 12 attempts to reach a decision-maker and if you're trying to access the C-Suite, expect to make at least 12 to 14 attempts.

Scott Stratten covers a tailor-made approach in his article on email campaigns. In it, he speaks to three different time sequences from three different studies. The first study indicated that the best window to send a well-timed email is between 12 a.m. – 3 a.m. The next study provided two windows between 8 a.m. – 10 a.m. and 3 p.m. – 4 p.m. And the final study cited identified the best window as being between 6 a.m. – 7 a.m.[24]

We are all guilty of confirmation bias and if you look hard enough you'll find an answer that reinforces your belief system. If you have a system in place that is working for you, constantly test and tweak it. But if you don't, it's time to write a new song or create a new playbook, using the following (and flexible) guidelines:

- Make between 8 and 14 attempts or touches before closing a file. Then circle back to that prospect in 6 to 12 months, if you have an infinite number of prospects.

- Keep in mind that a touch includes but is not limited to a voicemail, email, snail-mail letter, and/or a LinkedIn message.

- Remember to approach connecting as both an art and a science, taking both creative skill and a willingness to constantly re-evaluate (or test) that approach.

- Maintain a balance between being professionally persistent without being a pest or annoyance.

- Make an average of 2 touches a week, utilize emails/voicemails as a follow-up.

- Alternate your touches.

- Develop a series of readily available voicemails in addition to your intentionally planned emails.

Once you have set-up a system using the above guidelines, then you can easily follow the schedule below:

- Week 1: Send an email, follow up with a phone call, and send a direct mail piece (3 touches.)

- Week 2: Send an email, follow up with a phone call, and send LinkedIn Inmail (3 touches.)

- Week 3: Send an email and make a phone call (2 touches.)

- Week 4: Send an email, make a phone call, and send a handwritten note (3 touches.)

- Week 5: Send an email and unconventional gift to get attention (2 touches.)

If you follow this schedule to the letter, you will have made 13 touches in 5 weeks. Typically, I recommend that you should limit your touches to only once a week. For example, if you call someone on Monday, the earliest you should call them again is the following Monday. Ditto on emails and direct mail. The constant bombardment of a potential client will only come across as annoying and desperate.

In the end, remember your goal is to come across as professional and politely persistent. But Darren Saul cautions the sales professional from being too professional. Instead, he recommends being friendly. In his way of thinking, the word professional usually denotes an individual who is stiff, polished, guarded, unapproachable, and without a soul. Friendly identifies someone as authentic, fun, engaging, and a relationship builder. In everything, embrace friendly over robotic and impersonal.[25]

SCOREBOARD SUMMARY:

When writing (or rewriting) your company's song, keep it clear and concise but don't forget to also make it friendly. Read your prospect's social cues and take the first step to being vulnerable. Use humor without being cringeworthy. And remember, people will always crave authenticity over guarded professionalism.

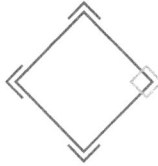

CHAPTER 16:
A Dream Marketer's Dilemma

"You're not responsible for the hand of cards you were dealt. You're responsible for maxing out what you were given." – Christopher Sommer

Inbound leads always require that you listen to your prospect, ask open-ended questions, assess his/her situation, and then diagnose the problem(s.) While one might assume this only pertains to those who have a few inbound leads, it also occurs when you have an abundance of leads as well. While the very suggestion that you can have too many inbound leads may leave you questioning my credibility and perhaps, my sanity, I have encountered clients who face the unusual challenge of having too many inbound leads. In terms of our baseball metaphor when you are given the grace of a head start or steal, use it wisely.

Not long ago, a software company out of Torrance, California, hired us to offer solutions for their marketing dilemma. With their marketing department generating over 1,200 inbound leads a month, they needed a system in place that prioritized leads and provided consistent follow-up. This is the case for most companies that have an overly robust marketing department. It is important to note here that inbound leads have different follow-up procedures than those that are outbound. For example, someone who fills out the "Contact Us" form is a higher priority than someone who simply downloaded a whitepaper.

When addressing an overwhelming influx of leads, it is important to step back and distinguish between suspect vs. prospect. A suspect is someone who raises his/her hand and says, "I'm interested in your product or services." A prospect is someone interested in your services and can afford you. Keep in mind that just because someone is interested in your services doesn't mean they can afford you or that you're the right fit for him/her. For example, I happen to love Maseratis. But that doesn't mean I have the budget to justify purchasing one. In this case, I would then be classified as a Maserati suspect rather than a qualified prospect.

In the case of my client who was overwhelmed with 1,200 monthly leads, this challenge provided a way of prioritizing certain prospects over others. A high-priority lead means anyone who comes to your website and fills out a contact form should receive a follow-up contact within 30-60 minutes. Research subsequently supports this kind of prioritization. Current data confirms that if you do not contact an inbound lead before it is 30 to 60 minutes old, the likelihood of converting it to a sales qualified lead plunges to zero. Hence, reaching out to leads by the end of the day will not work in terms of securing business.

An article from the Harvard Business Review found that firms who tried to contact potential customers within an hour of receiving a query were nearly seven times more likely to qualify a lead. Or in other words, the firms were seven times more likely to have a meaningful conversation with a decision-maker as those that try to contact a customer even an hour later and more than 60 times as likely as companies that contact them 24 hours or longer.[26]

"Nonetheless, our research indicates that many firms are too slow to follow up on these leads. We audited 2,241 U.S. companies, measuring how long each took to respond to a web-generated test lead. Although 37% responded to their lead within an hour, and 16% responded within one to 24 hours, 24%

took more than 24 hours—and 23% of the companies never responded at all. The average response time, among companies that responded within 30 days, was 42 hours." [27]

Another 3rd party researcher suggested that you contact a lead within 30 minutes to an hour. *"When you receive an inbound lead, Inside Sales allows you to engage the lead instantly. The data shows that if you do not contact an inbound lead before it is 30 minutes old, the likelihood of converting it to a Sales Qualified Lead (SQL) plunges to near zero. Reaching out to leads at the end of the day does not work."* [28]

When you receive an inbound lead, you must have a system in place to contact them within 30-60 minutes. Any follow up email correspondence should gently but firmly remind the prospect that they downloaded a white paper, requested a demo or trial, or they filled out a "Contact Us" form.

Likewise, phone and voicemail follow-up should always be consistent. If I am following up with a prospect, a follow-up voicemail might go along the lines of something like this, "Hey, Bob, Ray Ruecker with Connect 5000, I am following up on your contact us form request that you sent us about 20 minutes ago. Please call me back at <phone number.> Again, my phone number is <phone number.>"

Not only should you follow up with all queries by phone, but you should also follow up with email as well. Because a prospect may not be at his/her desk, an email combined with voicemail are the most surefire way to make sure that your follow-up is noticed. I have countless stories of prospects who have filled out the "contact us" form, sent it in and our representative reached out immediately but the prospect was nowhere to be found. Simply put, you shouldn't assume that they are going to be at their desk within your 30-60 minute follow-up timeframe. Always have a cadence and a series of phone calls and emails spaced out in case you do not reach your prospect on the first attempt.

The rationale supporting this approach is that if you take the time to figure out why the heck the prospect decided to stop what she was doing, reach out to you, and seek your help and expertise, you will also uncover what is working for you and what might not be in both your marketing and communication follow-up. Even if you've heard the same answer from other prospects, let them talk and get it out on the table. Never assume you know why they called. Think of it this way: we wouldn't like it if we visited the doctor and he prescribed a solution to our problems without asking a few questions first. Our prospects are no different.

Moreover, I would also recommend having a couple of open-ended questions handy in case the prospect forgot why she called you. They may have called several other competitors or you caught them when something else was on their mind. And if getting the conversation started is overly awkward, offer a one to a two-minute overview of your company and what problems you solve. Then gently ask:

(Prospect First Name), is _____ a problem?

Is _____ a challenge?

Is _____ a priority in solving this year?

Depending on how she answers, ask probing questions like:

"How so?" "Tell me more?" "How long has this gone on?"

Now imagine for a moment that a software company offers a 30-day trial before a prospect purchases the program. Depending on what they need, how many users, and what features are available to them, the prospect will likely want to chat with a company representative before investing in the program. An effective follow-up plan might look something like this.

Touch 1:

Automated email sample:

Subject Line: Follow Up and Invite from XYZ Software

Hi Prospect First Name,

Thank you for taking the time out of your busy schedule to download our (Product Name) 30-day trial.

XYZ Software develops innovative practice management software for professional services firms worldwide. We help simplify the way firms enter and use the information for time tracking, billing, and project management. This allows you to make informed decisions faster, improve productivity, and increase performance. With more than 300,000 users, XYZ software is trusted by numerous industry firms.

One of our team members will be contacting you shortly to schedule a live walk-through demonstration so that you can understand the full benefits of our platform.

Here's the link to sign up for a live demonstration: www.xyz.com

For instructions to install the program, please click here: _____

To contact us:

Sales - 800-800-8888 or email us at sales@xyz.com

Support - 800-800-8888 or email us at support@xyz.com

We look forward to connecting with you soon!

Sincerely,

The XYZ Team

(This sets the expectation early that a rep will be contacting them to qualify the opportunity to determine if they are a suspect or a prospect.)

Touch 2: (Use if you do not get the prospect live.)

Voicemail #1

Hi _____, this is _____ with XYZ Software. I hope you're doing well. You recently downloaded our 30-day trial on _____. I'd like to personally invite you to join a walk-through demonstration at your convenience. Please call me back at _____. I'll try you again in a few days if I haven't heard from you. Again my phone number is _____."

Touch 3:

Email #2

Subject Line: Follow Up

Hi Prospect First Name,

I know you're busy so I'll quickly get to the point.

I'm following up on the voicemail I recently left you.

You downloaded our 30-day trial from our website back on _____.

We help companies simplify the way they enter and use the information for time tracking, billing, and project management. This allows you to make informed decisions faster, improve productivity, and increase performance.

Are these areas a current challenge and priority in your company?

If so, you'd benefit from a live walk-through demonstration so that you can understand the full benefits of our platform.

Here's the link to sign up for a live demonstration: www.xyz.com/LiveDemo

I'll reach out to you soon in the next few days if I haven't heard from you.

Sincerely,

Sales Rep 1st Name

If no response: Wait 2 business days, make another phone call, or send another email.

Touch 4:

Voicemail #2

"Hi _____, this is _____ with XYZ Software. I'm following up on your recent XYZ download from _____. I hope you've had a chance to test the program. If you're looking to simplify the way your company enters and uses information for time tracking, billing, and project management, we may be able to help. I'd like to personally invite you to a walk-through demonstration at your convenience. Please call me back at _____. I'll try you again in a few days if I haven't heard from you. Again my phone number is _____".

Touch 5:

Email #2

Subject Line: Should we talk?

Hi Prospect First Name,

I hope you're doing well.

You downloaded our XYZ 30-day trial back on _____.

Have you had a chance to explore the program in depth?

Is simplifying the way your company enters and uses information for time tracking, billing, and project management a current challenge and priority?

Are you open to some new ideas on how to use our platform to make informed decisions faster, improve productivity, and increase performance?

If so, we should carve out some time to chat.

I'd like to personally invite you to a live walk-through demonstration so that you can understand the full benefits of our platform and ask unlimited questions.

Here's the link to sign up for a live demonstration: www.xyz.com/LiveDemo.asp

Or feel free to contact me to schedule a convenient time to view a live demonstration.

Sincerely,

Sales Rep 1st Name

If no response: Wait 3 business days, then make another phone call and send an email.

Touch 6

Voicemail 3:

"Hi _____, this is _____ with XYZ Software. You recently downloaded our 30-day trial on _____. I'd like to invite you to join a walk-through demonstration on how to use our platform to make informed decisions faster, improve productivity, and increase performance. Please call me back at _____. Again my phone number is _____".

Touch 7

Email 3:

Subject Line: Need more time?

Dear Prospect First Name,

I've left you a couple of voice messages and emails but have not heard back from you.

This typically means:

1. You've been busy, but are still very interested in talking with me about how I can help.

2. You would like me to follow up at a later date.

Being a business person, I know you can appreciate my position. I want to provide you with excellent client service and all of the information you require to make an educated decision that will benefit your business. What I don't want to do is bother you with my voicemails and emails.

Could you please help me by letting me know which of the two situations we are in?

This will allow me to better allocate my time while still providing you with the amount of attention you desire.

Sincerely,

Sales Rep 1st Name

If no response: Wait 5 business days, make a phone call, and then send an email.

Touch 8

Voicemail #4:

"Hi _____, this is _____ with XYZ Software. I'm following up on your recent XYZ 30-day trial. I've left you multiple messages and am having trouble connecting with you. I'd like to schedule a walk-through demonstration to review our platform at your convenience. Please call me back at _____. Again, my phone number is _____".

Touch 9

Email #4:

Subject Line: Should I stay or should I go?

Hi Prospect First Name,

It's been a while since we spoke.

I haven't heard back from you since you downloaded our 30-day trial on
_____ and that tells me one of three things:

1) You've already chosen another company for this and if that's the case
please let me know so can I stop bothering you.

2) You're still interested but haven't had the time to get back to me yet.

3) You've fallen and can't get up. In that case, please let me know and I'll
call 911 for you...

And let me know which one it is because I'm starting to worry.

Thanks in advance and I look forward to hearing back from you.

Sincerely,

Sales Rep 1st Name

If no response: Wait 7 business days, make a phone call, and then send an
email.

Touch 10

Voicemail #5

"Hi _____, this is _____ with XYZ Software. I have been unsuccessful
in my attempts to reach you and follow up on your 30-day trial. I'd like to
invite you to a walk-through demonstration to see our platform in more
detail. If I can assist you in any way, please call me at _____. Again my

phone number is _____. This is my final message and I'll remove you from our list unless I hear differently.

Touch 11

Email #5

Subject Line: XYZ Product Name - Still Interested?

Hi Prospect first name,

I hope you're doing well.

No one likes a "pesky" salesperson and I'm slightly concerned that I may be approaching that category with you.

Salespeople are conditioned since birth to be persistent. Ignoring us makes us dig our heels in deeper. (Yes, I know it makes no sense, but it is what it is).

If you've ever wanted a sure-fire way to shut down a salesperson and get rid of them for good, here are three ways that won't disappoint:

All options do not require a phone call; just an email response would do.

Option 1: Stop what you are doing and suggest a time that's convenient to schedule a walk-through demonstration.

Option 2: Let me know what's holding you back:

- Boss turned it down

- Budget / Too expensive

- Can't get everyone on board

- Timing isn't right

- Not sure this will really improve our current situation

Give me one final shot at offering a solution to these issues that might make you happy.

Option 3: You have already purchased another software program and are no longer interested in us.

Look forward to hearing from you soon.

Sincerely,

Sales Rep First Name

If you use the aforementioned sequence and receive no response, close the file and move on. Then reach out 6 months later unless it's a large company with an enormous revenue opportunity, or you've verified on LinkedIn that the decision-making executive is still with the company. The larger the organization, the harder it is to catch the appropriate decision-maker.

SCOREBOARD SUMMARY:
Even though inbound leads are easier to pursue than cold calls, prospects can still be elusive. Subsequently, having a cadence in play to follow up with inbound leads is vital. Whether the inquiry is for more information, the prospect downloaded a 30-day trial, or they simply want pricing, have a system in place. It is the best way to effectively and efficiently follow up with inbound leads and maximize connection.

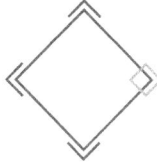

CHAPTER 17:
Reigniting a Cold Connection

"We have a strategic plan. It's called doing things." – Herb Kelleher

It happens all too often. You reach out to a prospect and he responds favorably by phone or email. He says he is interested in talking further but doesn't have access to his calendar. He asks you to follow up at a later time. You remain cautiously optimistic that you have made a quality connection. But then after repeated attempts to schedule a meeting, you are unsuccessful in connecting with your prospect. Simply put, you've been ghosted.

Several years ago, I attempted to connect with a $100M software company based in California. When I called the CEO's office, his assistant directed me to a certain Senior VP. I proceeded to call him and left a message referencing the assistant as my point of contact. After leaving 5 voicemails and 5 emails over 5 weeks, I closed the task in Salesforce.com. But ironically, the very next day the SVP called me back and we had a short discussion. Even though they had an inside sales team, he made it clear that he was not only interested in training but also made it a point to tell me that my timing couldn't have been better. We tentatively planned for me to fly out in the next two weeks with the understanding that we would firm up details by phone in two days.

But when I called back, his assistant answered. Once she heard why I had called, she explained that it was a no go for the next two weeks. Not only was their internal reorganization happening company-wide but the SVP's wife was also due to have a baby any day. Even though she recommended I call in March, I thought I was being blown off. But figuring I had nothing to lose, I followed up as she requested. When I finally connected live with the SVP's assistant, she revealed that it was no longer her boss's decision and to call the CMO. I reached out to the CMO a few times and referenced the SVP's name. He finally responded and we spoke by phone. During our conversation, I was able to give him an overview of the training workshops I conduct for companies nationwide.

Long story short, we agreed to terms and I flew out a few weeks later, conducted the workshop with 9 of the inside sales reps on how to make outbound prospecting calls, and put a system in place for future use. Not only was it a success, but it was also lucrative--I walked away making four figures for a day's worth of work. I share this not to brag but to encourage you. In total, it was an 8-month sales cycle, proving once again that the battle in this industry requires persistence, follow-up, and dedication to simply keep going even if it feels like home plate is out of reach.

When you get ghosted, an email/voicemail strategy to reconnect with a contact needs to be deliberate and purposeful. The following sample voicemail will give you a guide as to how to begin:

"Hi (Prospect's First Name,) Ray Ruecker with Connect 5000. We spoke on (specific date) about _____ and YOU requested I follow up with you to schedule some time on our calendars. Please call me back at (your phone number.) Again, my phone number is (your phone number.")

(The voicemail above can be an email touch as well.)

The above is short, sweet, and to the point and you're reminding your prospect that they requested a callback. Work diligently to space out your calls over different days and times. Also, complement the voicemails with carefully timed emails. Below are a few email templates I've used when a prospect goes dark on me.

Email #1
Subject Line: Quick Question
Prospect,

I still have you on my "waiting for" list of people from whom I am expecting to hear.

Am I still on your radar?
Ray

(That's it! This is after a few attempts of connecting with the prospect are unsuccessful.)

Email #2
Subject Line: Should I stay or should I go?
Paul,

It's been a while since we spoke.

I haven't heard back from you since April 27th and that tells me 1 of 3 things:

1) You've already chosen another company for this and if so, please tell me so can I stop bothering you.

2) You're still interested but haven't had the time to get back to me yet.

3) You've fallen and can't get up. And in that case, please let me know and I'll call 911 for you...

Please let me know which one it is because I'm starting to worry.

Thanks in advance and I look forward to hearing from you.
Ray

(Remember, you're in sales! Have some fun, use humor, and stand out!)

Email #3
Subject Line: Still Interested?
Prospect,

No one likes a pest and I'm slightly concerned that I may be approaching that category with you. I was conditioned since birth to be persistent. Ignoring me makes me dig my heels in deeper.

If you've ever wanted a sure-fire way to shut down a salesperson and get rid of them for good, here are 3 ways that won't disappoint: All options do not require a phone call, just an email response will do.

Option 1: Stop what you are doing and suggest a time that's convenient to continue our conversation.

Option 2: Let me know what's holding you back.
- Boss turned it down
- Budget / Too expensive
- Can't get everyone on board
- Timing isn't right
- Not sure this will really improve our current situation

Give me one final shot at offering a solution to these issues you may not have thought of but would make you happy.

Option 3: You've already chosen another provider and are no longer interested in Connect 5000.

I look forward to hearing from you soon.
Ray

(Help them say no. Prospects want to be liked and hate telling people no.)

Email #4
Subject Line: Quick Favor: A, B, or C
John,
I haven't heard from you in a while and hope everything is okay.

To make it easy, could you please respond with:

A. I've been busy, but I'll get back to you ASAP.

B. Snags with other priorities, so hang on and I'll get back to you soon.

C. We're going in a different direction. Thanks, but no thanks!

Thanks,

Ray

(Again, make it short, sweet and to the point and give the prospect an out.)

Email #5
Subject Line: Your company value proposition or subject of your conversation

Prospect,

Are you still thinking about _____ priority this year?

Ray

(This simple email reminds very busy prospects of your past conversation, and asks a very pointed question on their business pain, problem or challenge.)

Email #6
Subject Line: Final attempt to connect

Prospect First Name,
I've been unsuccessful in my attempts to reach you and follow up per your request.

This typically means one of two things:

1. You've been busy, but are still very interested in talking with me about how I can help.

2. You're no longer interested.

Being a business person, I hope you can appreciate my position. I want to provide you with excellent service and all of the information you require to make an educated decision that will benefit your business. What I don't want to do is bother you if you're no longer interested.

Could you please let me know which of the two situations we're in? This will allow me to better allocate my time while still providing you with the amount of attention you desire.

Thanks,

Ray

This is always my final email attempt. Stick to your guns and use this as a last resort. Just remember that voicemails and emails should respectfully remind your prospect that they requested you follow up with them. There's an infinite amount of reasons the prospect never called you back. But at this point, no matter if he/she was blowing you off or legitimately busy, close the file and move on to other prospects.

SCOREBOARD SUMMARY:
If you find yourself ghosted, begin by leaving a series of spaced-out voicemails and emails with the intent to reignite the conversation. But always remember that things come up in a prospect's life which also may explain his/her lack of correspondence. Be willing to accept this might be all that is keeping you from connecting. And while you should always be professionally persistent, don't shy away from being a little more open and vulnerable in your attempts to reopen the conversation.

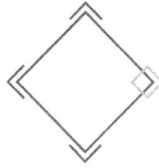

CHAPTER 18:
It's All in the Numbers

"What gets measured gets improved." – Peter Drucker, Management Guru

For most of my clients and prospects, they come to me not knowing how and what to measure. All too often, people think measurement means *complicated*, or they are measuring the wrong things (or even too many things.) But just like a batting average, tracking your numbers gives you/ your sales team a quantifiable way to measure improvement and set goals.

But let's step back for a moment. If you came to me because you were in debt and were trying to improve your financial situation, I would tell you to save more and spend less. But I would also tell you to write down every single item you purchased. From a pack of gum to a new car, I'd have you record every purchase because I'd know that with moment by moment awareness you would become more mindful of your purchases, and over time, your spending would go down.

Kristin Wong confirms this strategy in her book, *Get Money: Live the Life You Want, Not Just the Life You Can Afford*:

"I use good, old-fashioned pen and paper. I keep a small pocket notebook with me and write down my purchases. And I go a step further and I write down the stuff I'm tempted to buy, any notes about how I feel when I want to spend money impulsively, and any habits I notice. It sounds very touchy-feely, but learning to be good with money has so much to do with learning to manage your habits." [29]

But what does tracking your financial purchases have to do with sales accountability? Whatever you measure gets improved over time. Not overnight, mind you. *Over time.*

Countless business development folks long to do better when connecting or prospecting but are not entirely sure how to do it. Nor are they mindful of what tools they should use to improve. Instead, let's talk about only what is necessary--a simple tracking sheet using a fancy software program called Excel. When you are attempting to build a pipeline and establish an effective contact management system, it can feel overwhelming. But there is an old saying that begs the question, "How do you eat an elephant?" The answer? "One bite at a time." In other words, small steps are key to building and measuring success.

Begin by making reasonable goals and tracking them using Microsoft Excel. At Connect 5000, we track everything not only to provide personal accountability but to also measure productivity. The five sales metrics (or data) you should know and track at all times are:

1. How many sales calls did you make daily?

2. How many people did you catch live by phone or email?

3. How many conversations led to appointments or meetings?

4. How many proposals did you generate from those sales meetings?

5. How many proposals turned into new clients?

While I highly encourage you to use your company's CRM, know that there is intrinsic value in logging your results daily. Using these categories will ultimately allow you to track response ratios. The first three mentioned above identify what will fill the top of your sales funnel. But keep in mind that if you make a hundred phone calls in a day, expect 90% of those to go to voicemail. And if you talk to ten people, maybe 3-5 of them will say yes to a meeting. Because in the end, you want to set your goal at a 3% response ratio.

Now let me be clear, I am not advocating that you make a hundred phone calls a day. In the beginning, you will need to make your goals small and realistic. For example, at the beginning of the New Year, countless individuals want to get healthier so they make a resolution to lose weight, hit the gym five days a week, eat cleaner, and cut out alcohol. Not bad things. But trying to implement everything at once and accomplish it all can be overwhelming and is ultimately a recipe for disaster.

At Connect 5000, we use the following chart for tracking and accountability:

Terms
- Total Calls = all calls made to prospects
- Total Voicemails = all voicemails made to prospects
- Total Live Connects = all live conversations with prospects
- Total Set Meetings = all meetings set

Month (July)	Total		Week 1	1-Jul Monday	2-Jul Tuesday	3-Jul Wednesday	4-Jul Thursday	5-Jul Friday	Weekly Total		2	8-Jul Monday	9-Jul Tuesday	10-Jul Wednesday	11-Jul Thursday	12-Jul Friday	Weekly Total
Total Calls	0		Dials	0	0	0	0	0	0		Dials	0	0	0	0	0	0
Total Voicemails	0		VM	0	0	0	0	0	0		VM	0	0	0	0	0	0
Total Live Replies or Connec	0		Lives	0	0	0	0	0	0		Lives	0	0	0	0	0	0
Total Returned Calls	0		Lives	0	0	0	0	0	0		Lives	0	0	0	0	0	0
Total Set Meetings	0		Set Appointments	0	0	0	0	0	0		Set Appointments	0	0	0	0	0	0

Month (August)	Total		Week 6	5-Aug Monday	6-Aug Tuesday	7-Aug Wednesday	8-Aug Thursday	9-Aug Friday	Weekly Total		Week 7	12-Aug Monday	13-Aug Tuesday	14-Aug Wednesday	15-Aug Thursday	16-Aug Friday	Weekly Total
Total Calls	0		Dials	0	0	0	0	0	0		Dials	0	0	0	0	0	0
Total Voicemails	0		VM	0	0	0	0	0	0		VM	0	0	0	0	0	0
Total Live Replies or Connec	0		Lives	0	0	0	0	0	0		Lives	0	0	0	0	0	0
Total Returned Calls	0		Lives	0	0	0	0	0	0		Lives	0	0	0	0	0	0
Total Set Meetings	0		Set Appointments	0	0	0	0	0	0		Set Appointments	0	0	0	0	0	0

To download your copy, please visit my website at www.connect5000.com

Not only do I require all my team to fill this out, but they also send me a daily update of their numbers. I have this requirement for two reasons:

1. **Personal accountability.** If my reps know they have to turn this in daily, they are more likely to make their calls. Do I expect perfection? Absolutely not! Life doesn't exist in a vacuum and things come up. I expect them to have off days but in the long run, the productive days typically outnumber the bad.

2. **Professional statistics.** Each of my clients is different and wants to know what's required statistically so they can keep track internally. If ABC input spits out XYZ output, then my client can scale up and add both inside and outside reps to create a more predictable outcome. It helps with their financial forecasting as well. If the client is tracking sales closure rates somewhat accurately, then keeping track of the "top of the funnel" statistics is important too.

While there are a lot of tracking tools out there, keep it simple and begin with Excel. Add necessary categories relevant to you and your company without going over the top. But know that at the end of each day, you need to log your numbers and review them at the end of the week. Once you mastered your number of calls to make each day, look for trends and incrementally set higher goals.

For example, after a month, if you've consistently made 20 calls per day, move that goal to 30 calls per day. 15 before lunch and 15 after lunch. And so on. By the end of the month, you should get a picture of your progress and look for ways to improve. Add a second tab on the sheet for monthly totals so that at the end of the year, you'll have some good sales data to review and can make changes accordingly.

SCOREBOARD SUMMARY:

By tracking your numbers, you will be able to quantify what it takes to be successful daily. Begin with creating small and achievable goals. Once those are met, reassess your goals and push yourself further. This process will naturally move you toward the end game of scoring from first base.

CONCLUSION

The journey to first base (and beyond) may seem an arduous task. But if you use the framework provided in this book, you will make it all the way home, closing sales and landing new clients. Whether you are going through the process alone or you are passing the opportunity off to your sales team, you will have success if you follow my formula and cultivate consistency.

Be assured that this journey doesn't need to be complicated nor sophisticated. Life is challenging enough without making it harder. Don't overthink every recommendation and trust the process. Because in the end, lead generation and business development aren't about doing one thing right, it's about doing several things well. In a world oversaturated with information, we have more than enough sales tools. True success lies in selecting the most appropriate and beneficial tools for your business model.

With the right framework, anyone trying to achieve sales success can and will as long as what's built is tailored to one's individual needs. So, don't beat yourself up if you go through countless revisions and iterations to determine the best cadence for you and your company. Out of structure comes flexibility. And remember, if you want to cross home plate, you have to start on first base.

Happy connecting and swing for the fences!

Ray Ruecker

CONCLUSION

ADDITIONAL RESOURCES

A source is only as good as it's information. And in sales, while experience counts, understanding that the sales community provides a wealth of knowledge and a spirit of collaboration is just as important. While it might be tempting to stop learning, especially as we get busy and experience success, a commitment to excellence starts with a desire to learn, and a passion to better ourselves.

A former sales manager of mine owned this little saying, "If you're green, you're growing, but if you are ripe, you are rotting." That has stuck with me to this day. I'm an avid reader with 100 plus books on both my Kindle and Nook. In that spirit, this addendum provides some additional resources that have benefitted my sales career and may serve to sharpen your skills and reaffirm a commitment to learning:

168 Hours: You Have More Time Than You Think by Laura Vanderkam

The Accidental Sales Manager by Chris Lytle

Agile Selling by Jill Konrath

Close the Deal by Sam Deep and Lyle Sussman

Do it Marketing: 77 Instant Action Ideas to Boost Sales, Maximize Profits and Crush Your Competition by David Newman

Fanatical Prospecting by Jeb Blount

Grit: The Power of Passion and Perseverance by Angela Duckworth

High-Profit Prospecting by Mark Hunter

How to Get a Meeting with Anyone by Stu Heinecke

LinkedIn Riche$ by John Nemo

News Sales Simplified by Mike Weinberg

The Sales Advantage by Dale Carnegie and Associates

Sales Truths by Mike Weinberg

Selling to Big Companies by Jill Konrath

Selling to the C-Suite by Nicholas Read and Stephen J. Bistritz

Smart Calling: Eliminate the Fear, Failure, and Rejection from Cold Calling by Art Sobczak

Smart Selling on the Phone and Online by Josiane Chriqui Feigon

SNAP Selling by Jill Konrath

Take the Cold Out of Cold Calling by Sam Richter

Time Management by Brian Tracy

Value Forward Selling by Paul DiModica

NOTES

Introduction

[1] https://adage.com/article/cmo-strategy/lowdown-report-cmos-half-tenure-ceos/307992

Chapter 2

[2] https://www.statista.com/statistics/264810/number-of-monthly-active-facebook-users-worldwide

[3] https://www.oberlo.com/blog/linkedin-statistics

[4] https://www.oberlo.com/blog/twitter-statistics

[5] https://www.omnicoreagency.com/pinterest-statistics

[6] https://growthbadger.com/blog-stats

[7] https://businessesgrow.com/2014/01/06/content-shock

[8] https://go.roberts.edu/leadingedge/the-great-choices-of-strategic-leaders

[9] https://www.redcrowmarketing.com/2015/09/10/many-ads-see-one-day

[10] https://time.com/3858309/attention-spans-goldfish/

[11] https://blog.sanebox.com/2016/02/18/email-overload-research-statistics-sanebox/

Chapter 3

[12] http://www.insidesales.com/insider/dialer/4-sales-tips-for-making-contact-and-avoiding-prospect-badgering/

[13] Art Sobczak. Smart Calling: Eliminate the Fear, Failure, and Rejection from Cold Calling. New Jersey: Wiley Publishing, 2013.

[14] http://www2.discoverorg.com/e/10192/huffingtonpost/29p4b2/427614601

Chapter 4

[15] https://www.amazon.com/Dr-Stephen-J-Bistritz-ebook/dp/B002N-2JLLW/ref=sr_1_3?dchild=1&keywords=selling+to+the+c+-suite&qid=1592858899&sr=8-3

[16] https://www.amazon.com/Dr-Stephen-J-Bistritz-ebook/dp/B002N-2JLLW/ref=sr_1_3?dchild=1&keywords=selling+to+the+c+-suite&qid=1592858899&sr=8-3

Chapter 6

[17] https://neilpatel.com/blog/direct-mail-effectiveness

Chapter 7

[18] http://www.rainsalestraining.com/blog/sales-prospecting-guidelines

[19] https://www.business2community.com/b2b-marketing/b2b-lead-qualification-bant-obsolete-0723256

Chapter 8

[20] https://www.skipprichard.com/3-tips-for-more-effective-email/

[21] https://cdn2.hubspot.net/hub/110248/file-16527786-pdf/documents/ultimateguide-emailprospecting.pdf

Chapter 12

[22] https://www.businessinsider.com/how-lebron-james-spends-money-body-care-2018-7#:~:text=James%20is%20said%20to%20spend,chefs%2C%20appliances%2C%20and%20more

Chapter 14

[23] Hunter, Mark. High-Profit Prospecting: Powerful Strategies to Find the Best Leads and Drive Breakthrough Sales Results. New York: American Management Association, 2017.

Chapter 15

[24] http://www.unmarketing.com/2013/01/21/the-best-time-to-never-send-email

[25] http://saulrecruitment.blogspot.com/2011/02/professional-or-friendly-or-both-by.html?m=1

Chapter 16

[26] Oldroyd, James B. et al. Harvard Business Review, "The Short Life of Online Sales Leads." March 2011.

[27] http://hbr.org/2011/03/the-short-life-of-online-sales-leads/ar/1

[28] https://salesbenchmarkindex.com/insights/your-customers-are-telling-you-to-reconsider-inside-sales

Chapter 18

[29] Wong, Kristin. Get Money: Live the Life You Want, Not Just the Life You Can Afford. New York: Hachette Book Group, 2018.

NOTES

ACKNOWLEDGMENTS

Writing a book has been on my bucket list for as long as I can remember. But like so many other things, it fell into the "someday" category until the Fall of 2018, when I casually mentioned my goal to my long-time friend, Stacy Stephens. With her encouragement and introduction to her friend and editor, Sara, my dream became reality. As with most worthwhile dreams, many friends, colleagues, and family members helped mine come to fruition. So, indulge me a moment while I take the time to express my gratitude:

To my dad, Arnold Ruecker II, thank you will never be enough. Your heart and deep capacity to love gave me a chance at life and the opportunity to call you family. Your words "Apply yourself!" always find me in moments where I feel like giving up. Your example of what it means to be a provider, husband, and father is one I will always strive to emulate. And even though you went home to heaven nearly five years ago, your love is in everything I do.

To my mom, Fran Ruecker, my love and admiration for you only continue to grow as I parent my son and daughter. I am often left to wonder how you raised so many kids with such patience and love. Thank you for choosing me and loving me as your own. Thank you for always encouraging me. And thank you for your guidance in both the little and big things in life. I love you!

To my wife, Kate Ruecker, my beautiful bride, and the ultimate proof I can sell, I love you more than I will ever be able to express. Thank you for supporting me through all the ups and downs of being an entrepreneur. Thank you for giving me two wonderful, bright, and resourceful children. And thank you for loving me in the middle of all life's chaos. May we never adopt a puppy during a pandemic again!

To my children, Olivia and William, I love you forever and am beyond proud to be your dad.

To A.B.R: cheers, blessings, and love!

To my siblings, Dayna, Arnie, Katie, Wendi, Lyndelle, Anthony, Tamorah, Breanne, Karen, Jessica, and their extended family, thank you for your lifelong support and love.

To my in-laws, Bill, Ruth, John, Elizabeth, and their extended family, thank you for welcoming me into the family and giving me the chance to love and be loved by Kate.

To Stacy Stephens, thank you for 30 years of good conversation, memories, and friendship. You have been instrumental in making this dream of mine become a reality through your encouragement and introduction to Sara. But most of all, thank you for letting me return the favor by cheering you on as you launch your firm and chase your dreams. I am so proud of you.

To my word maestro, Sara Cormany, thank you for all you did to make this book come to fruition, as well as holding up your end of the bargain to not die before the manuscript was finished. It was an absolute pleasure to laugh, collaborate, and finish this together.

To Matthew Richey, my best friend since 1999, thank you for sticking closer than a brother and walking through life with me. (Remember, bald is fashionable and always in.)

To Phil Buccero, my other best friend since 2000, thank you for always being kind, thoughtful, and full of wisdom. It is a privilege to call you friend.

To Bridget Alexander, Shawn Beldin, Lance Cleaver, Gary Greenlaw, Matt Heelan, Ron Light, Derek Lindberg, Alex Miller, Heather Tucker, Sonja Walker, Liz Wilson, Whitney Wilson, and Larry Wilcox, thank you for offering your friendship in the various times and seasons I needed it.

To my friends and fellow entrepreneurs, Noman Ahmad, Gabe Barnes, Brandy Branstetter, Brad Burrow, Anthony Casarona, Ed Gandia, Brenda Heffron, Michael Katz, Debra Kunz, Cynthia Kyriazis, Craig McElvain, Alana Muller, Mark Romero, Christy Rogers, Keith Sciulli, Marc Shaffer, John Stevenson, and Gail Tolbert, thank you for always inspiring me.

To my team at Connect 5000, both past and present, Danita Regehr, who's kept me on track from day one, Patti Mbachu, who's impressed me since our first interview ten years ago, Anne Brown, Deb Finley, Linda Gibson, Nisah Howard, Ron Jaramillo, Tiffany Miller, Boni Newberry, John Pannebaker, Patti Mbachu, Hanna Rodriguez, and Mike Smiley, thank you for your faithful commitment to our company's mission.

To my friends, Chris Bell, Atchison Frazer, Gary Greenberger, Gretchen Hoffman, Ron Sloop, Adam Stein, Byron Whetstone, and others who I initially met as Connect 5000 clients, thank you for mentoring me, inspiring me, and partnering with me.

To all my Connect 5000 clients, thank you for the opportunity to work with your sales organization. Working together has allowed me to broaden and deepen my expertise. I couldn't be where I am today without you.

To the many authors, entrepreneurs, and thinkers who contributed to this book directly and indirectly--leaders like Jeb Blount, Mark Hunter, Anthony Iannarino, Jill Konrath, John Nemo, Art Sobczak, and Mike Weinberg, thank you for the continued education.

And to those I may have inadvertently and mistakenly left off the list, those who have greatly impacted my life and who I didn't intend to exclude, know

ACKNOWLEDGMENTS

I'm grateful for you. Thank you for all the love, encouragement, and support.

Last but certainly not least, to Jesus Christ, my personal Lord and Savior, may I always live within the truth that apart from you, I can do nothing.

*I am the vine; you are the branches. If you remain in me
and I in you, you will bear much fruit; apart from me,
you can do nothing.*

JOHN 15:5

ABOUT THE AUTHOR

Ray Ruecker is the Managing Director of Connect 5000, a Kansas City-based lead generation, prospecting training, and sales consulting company. Since March 2010, Connect 5000 has helped countless software, technology, and consulting companies boost sales revenue with effective lead generation campaigns, sales prospecting strategies, and inside sales management. In addition to providing support to existing company leadership, Ray has also served as an interim sales leader for firms until they find a permanent solution.

Ray holds two Bachelor degrees from Washburn University in Business Administration with an emphasis in marketing and management. Born in Saigon, Vietnam, and raised in the rural Midwest, Ray now lives in the Kansas City metro with his wife, Kate, their two children, Olivia and William, and their mischievous Goldendoodle, Millie.

Connect with Ray at https://www.linkedin.com/in/rayruecker/.

Check out his blog at http://www.connect5000.com/blog/.

View his video blog at http://www.connect5000.com/videos/.

Follow him on Twitter @RayRuecker.

www.ingramcontent.com/pod-product-compliance
Lightning Source LLC
Chambersburg PA
CBHW061732020426
42331CB00006B/1207